Forbes®

GREAT MINDS OF BUSINESS

Forbes®

GREAT MINDS OF BUSINESS

COMPANION TO THE PUBLIC TELEVISION SERIES

FORBES INC.

GRETCHEN MORGENSON,
SENIOR EDITOR

John Wiley & Sons, Inc.
New York • Chichester • Weinheim • Brisbane • Singapore • Toronto

Library of Congress Cataloging in Publication Data:
ISBN 0-471-19652-5

Printed in the United States of America

10 9 8 7 6 5 4 3 2 1

CONTENTS

Forbes®
GREAT MINDS OF BUSINESS

ANDREW GROVE

CONTENTS

CONTENTS

FOREWORD

What is the key to business success? That question has animated FORBES magazine since its beginnings 80 years ago. At its most fundamental, the answer today is the same as it was then: *leadership.*

Take the measure of the people at the top of a business and you will get a clearer sense of that company's prospects than from its balance sheet, profitability, cash flow, market share, and market capitalization. The people matter most, and accounting cannot quantify their value. Similarly, the drama of business is not in the numbers or in the recitation of dry fact. It lies in the people who made and make it happen.

The early issues of the magazine conveyed this idea with a simple subhead attached to the title: FORBES Devoted to Doers and Doings. This collection of interviews—created as a companion to the public television series of the same name—is a natural descendant of that view. Talking with top knockers about specific dimensions of their businesses is a superb way to learn the art and craft of management. It is also a marvelous way to feel the excitement and pulse, the real drama of running and building a business.

Just listen to Fred Smith of Federal Express on how he used information and technology to build his business. How did Pleasant Rowland develop a brilliant marketing plan that was based on her own passions, rather than focus-group feedback? What was it like to be at the center of the Pentium crisis at Intel? Where did Peter Lynch get his best ideas in running one of the most successful mutual funds in history? How did Paul Volcker tame the worst American inflation since the Civil War?

Andy Grove, Fred Smith, Peter Lynch, Pleasant Rowland, and Paul Volcker are truly "Great Minds of Business." They have all made enormous direct contributions to business and the economy. They also embody ideas and virtues that we can all learn from. Each has followed a very different path to success, but one of the common threads is *failure*. They have endured adversity and had the strength to learn from it and move forward. At moments when others might have given in to pessimism and despair, they did not.

Today, optimism reigns in America and much of the rest of the world, and with good reason. The business prospects appear bright. Arguably, they are brighter than ever before. But no mood lasts indefinitely. Since that first issue of FORBES appeared in September 1917, the world has seen wars and revolutions, depression, inflations, and recessions too numerous to recount. The mood of the moment has moved accordingly. Undoubtedly, the business outlook will darken again one day. When it does, remember these people and what they have to say. They were making their successes through bad times as well as good.

Timothy C. Forbes
August 1997

INTRODUCTION

What does it take to make it in today's feverishly paced, ferociously competitive business world? And do I have it?

These are probably the two most common questions posed by people in business today. Anyone who wants to be around and competing next week or next year has to ask constantly: Do I have what it takes to remain in the game? Across industries and regardless of level of experience—managers, investors, marketers, and entrepreneurs—the question applies to all, because, in the combat zone that is business today, anyone can be blown away by a competitor, even a colleague. Gone are the days of employment for life in one comfortable, predictable corporation.

And yet, even with all this competition, today's business environment is a dichotomy. It is an era of extremes, not unlike the stage Charles Dickens set in *A Tale of Two Cities*—the best of times, the worst of times.

On one hand, the opportunities for success on an enormous scale for enormous numbers of people have never been greater than they are in our computer age. Thanks to the silicon chip, it is now not only possible but also relatively simple for an entrepreneur to sell goods or services to customers in the most remote corners of the world. Efficiencies in any operation can be honed with a computer, ideas can be implemented more quickly than ever before, information and the power that comes with it can be dispensed to millions of people instantaneously. The world has, in effect, shrunk to a size that makes products sold by Coca-Cola, GAP, Phillip Morris, and Tiffany almost as ubiquitous in Tibet as they are in Toledo. All thanks to the computer and the silicon chip.

But there's a downside to this widening marketplace, a negative that accompanies all that potential, a view that says the cup is half empty. This is the sobering reality—that along with the winners, there will also be losers. Folks who, for whatever reason, cannot make the transition from the old way to the new, people who don't know how to leap across the chasm of massive change. It's inevitable: For many people, a changing of the guard brings dislocation, disruption, fear, and paranoia.

And so in one column of the newspaper we read about the ever increasing number of billionaires in the world. In 1991, according to FORBES magazine, there were 274 people in the world who were worth at least $1 billion. Five years later there were almost twice as many—entrepreneurs made fabulously wealthy and famous, seemingly overnight, by implementing a great idea. To which many of us respond, "Why didn't I think of that?"

But adjacent to that story is another, more dismal tale. This one is about thousands of people being laid off at corporations across the country, people made obsolete by their computer or their competitor. The downsized. The ones left behind. Best of times, worst of times.

Indeed, the contemporary business arena is filled with potential, yet fraught with peril. We know we're at the edge of a new century and on the cusp of huge change. And so we wonder, all the more, if we have what it takes to make it in today's perilous business world. Knowing how easy it is to be one of those left behind makes the question seem more urgent every day.

Although all this uncertainty feels alarmingly new, America has been this way before. The winds of change sweeping across the horizon today are very reminiscent of another period in American history—where the development of a new product meant that the landscape would be changed forever. That period was the early 1900s and the product in development was the automobile.

Think about the similarities between then and now. The automobile, invented in 1885 in Mannheim, Germany by Karl-Friedrich Benz, had the potential to change the world; certainly it would transform consumers' lives if it were made accessible. But as is true with any revolutionary idea, early on it was almost impossible to quantify how big the demand for automobiles would ultimately be.

Nevertheless, entrepreneurs rushed in to try to grab a piece of the action. In the 1910s, there were some 300 different car manufacturers in the United States, all producing their own version of the horseless buggy. Hundreds of ancillary businesses sprang up to supply the nascent car industry with parts—tiremakers and headlamp manufacturers, for example—producing opportunities for those entrepreneurs. The automobile was undoubtedly a product with great promise. But how much acceptance would it gain? Very hard to quantify.

Until Henry Ford came along. Ford, in designing a way to mass-produce cars—the assembly line—was able to reduce vastly the costs of manufacturing his Model T. Passing along some of those cost savings to car buyers ensured that the Ford auto would be a huge hit. And so it was.

So it is today with the computer industry. Everyone agrees that computers and the Internet will change lives around the world—they already have to a small degree. What is unknown is just how widespread consumer acceptance of computers will be. As was true with the burgeoning automobile industry, hundreds of computer makers, software writers, networking companies, Internet providers, modem manufacturers, and other suppliers of ancillary gear have jumped into the market-place. Will they all survive? No way. Only three of the 300 American car makers survived that industry's shakeout. Similar odds face manufacturers of information technology products right now.

For the computer to become truly ubiquitous, somebody needs to figure out a way to make computing more affordable than it currently is; such was the case in the fledgling auto industry. That is the essential challenge facing computer manu-facturers—and the companies who supply them. In the mean-time, managers, retailers, investors, even computer buyers wonder: Who will survive and who will fall by the wayside?

The $64 billion question. If it were answerable, everyone would be a billionaire and no one would be laid off. Everyone would win, no one would lose. Back on planet Earth, however, we're all wondering how to make sure we won't be the next casualty. What does it take to succeed today? Even in this time of extreme change the clues are there. Some are obvious: Hard work. Determination. Luck. Guts. Others are not. Getting be-yond these basics—to get genuine insights that can help you right now—you have to ask the right people. Who?

We could start by polling all those freshly minted billionaires for our answers. But being wealthy, although a goal for many, is not a singular enough achievement. Besides, today's billionaires very often are not tomorrow's. Between 1990 and 1995, for example, 98 individuals dropped off the Forbes 400 list of richest Americans because their fortunes faded away. Like everything else about our lives that has speeded up in recent years, fortunes rise and fall faster today. Even a billion dollars can be evanescent.

No, the best candidates to ask about success and how it is derived today are people whose accomplishments have taken them to a level of success unmatched in their fields. People who have thrived even in our era of immense transition. Folks who've been at the top of their game long enough to know that their success is not a fluke. Who know how to stay on top.

This is extremely important in an era roiled by transformation. Given the quickened pace of change in today's world of business, the people who are successful year in, year out, are rare indeed. So the best folks to ask about achieving success and hanging on to it today are people who have themselves wrought significant change on the business world. Want to know how to survive and thrive during times of change? Who better to ask than the changemakers? The people best able to tell the rest of us how to stay ahead of the curve. The great minds of business.

Who are these great business minds? Who are the contemporary equivalents of oil magnate John D. Rockefeller, financier J. P. Morgan, IBM founder Thomas Watson, steel genius Andrew Carnegie? And what does it mean to be a great mind of business? For starters, such a person needs to have known and overcome adversity: Facing down failure and emerging even the stronger for the encounter is a prerequisite of business success, especially now. A great mind of business would also need a keen understanding of human nature: No achiever gets to the summit without help from others. Another characteristic common to the greatest minds of business is flexibility, a talent for rolling with the punches. Add this paramount requirement: a one hundred thousand percent commitment to the business goal.

To identify today's great business minds, FORBES searched a cross section of industries, looking specifically for men and women leading the charge in each of the following five categories: management, entrepreneurship, investing, marketing, and finance. How did we select our five business categories? Although they all overlap to some degree—entrepreneurship is probably a requirement of any successful businessperson, regardless of industry—they are five discrete arenas of business in which a person who wants to succeed must excel.

Looking for our leaders, we considered the famous, we considered the obscure. Age was irrelevant, wisdom required. The most significant hurdle that had to be cleared: Each individual had to have changed the way American business is conducted. This narrowed the field substantially. Only a very few business people have genuinely changed the way American business is done.

The result is a most interesting list. Of our five choices, some are household names, others are not. Their stories may surprise you; their wisdom will inspire.

➤ ➤ ➤

Our guru on management is a sixty-three-year-old Hungarian émigré who arrived in the United States in 1956 with neither a word of English nor a dime in his pocket. Today he runs the company that makes the semiconductor chips that power 90% of the world's personal computers. He is Andrew Grove, chairman, CEO, and co-founder of Intel, the San Jose–based giant in semiconductor chip manufacturing. Grove is widely viewed as the best corporate manager in America, if not the world. His company employs 40,000 people, has had operating profit margins of at least 31% since 1990, and has seen its sales rise 15-fold since 1986. Intel stock has rewarded investors by rising from $7-a-share in 1990 to a recent $165. Investors who bought shares of Intel when the company came public in 1975 paid just 6 cents per share, adjusted for splits.

A dialogue with Grove reveals much about how to manage for success. Grove is a man upon which much of our computer and communications age is built, a man responsible for taking America headlong into the future. Yet he maintains that when he helped found Intel in 1968, he spent not one moment thinking about what lay ahead. "I was 32 years old," he recalls. "I was worried about whether we were able to produce a product. I was looking very much down at my toes and the next pebble that was going to trip us. It was one step at a time."

As it turned out, Grove was wise to be wary. The pebbles were very much there. As you'll see, his story is not one glory after the next. In just the past 15 years, Grove has experienced several harrowing times that threatened Intel's very existence— dark days when all that he and his team had invested in the company and worked for over decades could have come to naught. He speaks openly about these fearsome times. One of the worst? In 1985, came an invasion of Japanese chipmakers able to produce for far less money the same kind of memory chips made by Intel and other American manufacturers. This episode almost cost Intel its life as a public company—it bled money for two years and flirted with bankruptcy.

How Grove righted his company is an amazing tale achieved by real, outside-the-box thinking on Grove's part. And today, when Intel's scenario could not be rosier, Grove is by no means comfortable. This man, indisputably at the pinnacle of management success, lives in constant fear that disaster will again hit his company. "Am I comfortable that something like this couldn't happen again?" he asks. "No. I have no intention of lulling myself into comfort."

What's Grove worried about now? "Even more insidious is when something goes out of the market, something goes out of the technology. The vitality gradually disappears, so it's not even something that somebody else does to you; it's even more subtle. I worry about those things. I worry about maintaining the engine."

A philosopher, Grove has clearly done a good deal of thinking about the big issues facing managers today. He spells out his views on the current state of American business, vis-à-vis the world. He reveals what he believes is the biggest battle that managers must fight—not a fight with a competitor, but a battle with oneself against what Grove calls comfortable equilibrium, a.k.a. the status quo.

Part of Grove's management success is his insistence on analyzing failure. Says he: "There is a tendency to walk away from failure and leave it buried. There's an enormous amount of institutional learning that gets lost because failures don't get analyzed. So the real learning is in actual fact in the failure because something didn't work."

Not easy. But nothing that achieves the spectacular results that Grove has could be expected to be easy.

Andy Grove is a rare combination: an executive who is also an intellectual; a visionary who admits to not knowing what the next big thing in his industry will be; a man who has achieved practically unmatched success, yet who is always afraid.

❧ ❧ ❧

The entrepreneurial mastermind of business is a man who, more than any other entrepreneur in recent history, has physically changed the way business is done. His company, which did not exist a generation ago, has become so ubiquitous that its name is a verb, not only in English but in other languages, such as Chinese and Japanese. Not often that a man who invents a new company invents a new word as well.

Fred Smith, the founder and chairman of Federal Express Inc., conceived of a company that would guarantee delivery of a package from New York to California overnight for $8. Smith is also a man who, pursuing his liberal arts degree from Yale University, received a "C" from his economics professor on the paper outlining the idea that would later become Federal Express. Fred Smith, whose company is now the $11 billion giant in express delivery services, not only built a company, he built an entire $20-billion-plus industry. That's what the half-dozen, privately held express delivery services generated in revenues last year.

Federal Express employs 120,000 people in 200 nations around the world. Its stock has gone from a split-adjusted $3 when it came public in April 1978 to a recent $51. Its sales have almost quadrupled in the past ten years. On a typical business day, FedEx transports 2 million pounds of packages. Its well-honed system sorts 32 pieces of mail per minute.

Smith's particular genius is that he was the first person to see a monumental change afoot and to meet the needs that the change would bring. What did he see? The computer. What Smith recognized on the horizon in the mid-1960s was this: The computer was going to bring the kind of change to business and industry that would require extremely fast delivery systems to all the corners of the earth.

If the insight itself was enormous, meeting the challenge of it was monumental. So monumental, in fact, that Smith, looking back at it, says: "It was the classic case of not knowing what you're getting into or you wouldn't have done it."

What kind of a man has what it takes to envision and then build an entire industry? Once again, we see the complexities and dichotomies in Smith that are almost always found in high achievers. He describes himself as someone who flaunts authority, yet he served two tours of duty as a Marine in the Vietnam war. A man who says he is not a technology expert, but whose company is one of the best at adapting new technologies to bring even greater efficiencies to their customers. An excellent student who is also a world-class teacher.

Finally, Smith is one of that very rare breed: the inventor who also excels at managing the giant company his entrepreneurial venture has become. Not just a creator, but a leader as well.

What are, in Smith's view, the characteristics that a successful entrepreneur must have? To Smith, anyone who wants to build an enterprise must be part salesman, risk manager, capital raiser, disciplinarian, and leader. But first you've got to have an idea that's big enough with broad enough appeal. How do you come up with such an idea that no one else has thought of yet? "If you look at the history of most entrepreneurial ideas," Smith says, "there's that common denominator that somebody had a different perspective or slightly different view of something than the traditional wisdom or the traditional thinking was at the time."

Is such nontraditional thinking innate or can it be learned? Smith believes that it can be taught, and explains why.

As for his own challenge, Smith humbly says that if he had started Federal Express five years earlier it wouldn't have worked and five years later it would have been so obvious that there would have been insurmountable competition. Entrepreneurs who are right now contemplating how to implement their own big idea will be happy to hear Smith's view of today's entrepreneurial environment. Stated simply, Smith believes the years ahead will be "the greatest time ever for entrepreneurs." Go after it.

➤ ➤ ➤

Our third conversation is with a man who managed a mutual fund so successfully for 13 years that he outperformed all the stock market averages at least fivefold. This overachieving investor began honing his skills not in a money management training program, but as an 11-year-old caddy on a Boston area golf course. This "training" began in the 1960s, during a go-go stock market when he was in the position to overhear the casual investing talk of a handful of golfers.

Peter Lynch, famed Fidelity Magellan fund manager, bought his first stock—$900 worth of Flying Tiger Airlines—when he was a freshman on scholarship at Boston College. The stock went from $8 to $80 and paid for his MBA earned years later at the University of Pennsylvania's Wharton School of Business. "I made a lot of mistakes, too," Lynch concedes. "But that one was lucky. It worked."

Since retiring from the helm of the Fidelity Magellan Fund in 1990 at the age of 46, Lynch has written three books about investing and speaks regularly on the subject. He has become almost as famous an investing teacher as he was an investment manager. Perhaps this isn't surprising: He is the son of a Boston College professor who died when Lynch was 10.

Investors interested in improving their results can learn much from Lynch. His main belief is this: Individual investors can use their own life experiences and knowledge to pick promising stocks. And if they hold on to them, they can get wealthy. For people worried that they don't have the mind for the market, Lynch says: "The key organ here is the stomach. Are people ready for the declines? Because when the market declines, usually the background noise is not positive. People are being laid off, sometimes real estate prices are weak, or there are political problems."

For a man who was one of Wall Street's best stockpickers, Lynch is refreshingly open about his investment mistakes. He says: "I've been lucky enough to have some stocks that went up ten-, twentyfold. They were surprises. The ones where I said: 'Wow! If this works I'm going to make twentyfold, I've never broken even.' " In the heat of the stock-market moment, it's easy to get carried away, Lynch recognizes. But his insights can bring investors back down to Earth where, when all is said and done, the real money is made.

▸ ▸ ▸

In the pantheon of American marketing successes, one woman stands out. Not for the amount of money she makes on her product or for its uniqueness. Rather, this Wisconsin woman stands out for two reasons: With no experience in the toy business, she figured out how to sell $250 million worth of books and dolls to American girls not from the inside of a toy store, but from the inside of a mailbox.

More than anything else, the story of Pleasant Rowland, creator of The American Girls Collection and founder of Pleasant Rowland, is the story of a woman who had an idea she believed in. Simply put, Pleasant Rowland's passion ensured her success. Even as she broke all the rules typically found in business school marketing books.

Rowland may have broken all the rules because she didn't know what they were. "If I'd had an MBA," she chuckles, "I suppose I would have done things a lot differently. I probably wouldn't have believed that I could have done it."

This marketing eminence inherited crucial merchandising genes from her father. Although he didn't live to see his daughter's success, Rowland's father, an advertising executive in Chicago, said: "Great advertising is created in the detail."

Her attention to detail may have been one of the key characteristics that helped Rowland beat the well-capitalized giants in the toy business—Mattel and Hasbro, for example—at their own game. How did she do it, given that she had no advertising dollars to compete with to get her product on the radar screen? An interesting tale.

This marketing success believes she is not in the toy business, the doll business, or the book business. "I'm in the little girl business," she says. "We were really the first people to take this audience of girls, seven to twelve, seriously. Being for girls was the purpose, is still the purpose." This is the essence of Pleasant Rowland.

Now that Rowland's marketing success is unquestioned, she has to worry about new competition coming in to try to knock off her idea. "The more the merrier," she says. "We take a huge pride in having made a difference. And we want to continue making that difference. If the competition can match us, then the world is better for having more good stuff. But in the meantime, we're going to do our thing as well as we can."

Which is to say, well indeed.

➤ ➤ ➤

Who, more than any other single person, laid the groundwork for the biggest, wealth-creating bull market in stocks the United States has ever known? The modest son of a crusading city manager in Teaneck, New Jersey, and a self-effacing homemaker: Paul Volcker, Federal Reserve Chairman from 1979 to 1987. A man who devoted almost his entire career to public service, bringing to his work a credibility and integrity uncommon in the public sector today. An apolitical being who was thrust constantly into political fights. A man who served at the behest of two presidents, but who always felt he was working for the individual American.

A thoughtful man with a keen grasp of both American history and the history of money, Volcker is well aware of the threats to financial stability that lurk around every corner in this country and the world at large. This, even though we currently enjoy a healthy economy and have witnessed a rip-roaring stock market.

Volcker is now in the private sector, a vice chairman of banking giant Bankers Trust in New York City. He also teaches economics at Princeton University one day a week. He is the author of three books on economics and public policy. And he is heading up the task force designated to return money that belongs to the families of Holocaust victims secretly held for the past 40 years in Swiss bank accounts.

For all the public exposure he received as chairman of the Federal Reserve, Volcker remains a very private man. He opens up here, discussing his parents and siblings, his youth spent fishing and idolizing his Frank Capra-esque father. Mr. Volcker Goes To Washington, indeed.

As became obvious much later, Volcker was the man who, in the early 1980s, broke the back of the inflation that had dogged and decimated the American economy since 1975. And, by killing off that crippling inflation, Volcker laid the foundation for the biggest bull market in American history. In 1982, the Dow Jones industrial average stood at 821. Fifteen years later, it's near 8,000.

Volcker laughs off the idea that he is the father of the massive move in equities. He's far too modest and far too conservative to believe such a thing. But it is true, in this way: Had he not reduced inflation in the U.S., the stock market would not have performed as astoundingly as it subsequently did. Plain and simple.

A conversation with Paul Volcker is wide-ranging. Issues of concern to him include the world's need for capital, the disturbing impact of speculators in world markets, the cynical view of government which many Americans hold today. Volcker is also deeply worried about the low savings rate in the United States, our government deficits, and the future of Social Security. He warns of the dangers lurking in today's conventional wisdom that inflation is gone for good. Talking with Paul Volcker, the most famous of the fourteen Federal Reserve chairmen in American history, is a rare encounter with a brilliant mind.

❦ ❦ ❦

Great minds of business, all of them. Inauspicious in their beginnings, surprised at their own success perhaps, but five remarkable people. Individuals whose genius went unrecognized at first, but who proved up to the challenge of taking big, contrary business ideas from fantasy to reality. And doing so with all the attendant setbacks, obstacles, and adversity. Five people whose stories tell us what it takes to be exceptional, to be successful, to be an architect of monumental business change. Interestingly, not one of these five achievers set out to get rich with their ideas. Yet all are wealthy. Few actually set out to change the way American business is done. Yet that is what each one did. Such are the dichotomies that characterize success in the business world today.

Completely in character, none of the five individuals speaking on the following pages has decided to rest on his or her accomplishments. Each one is pushing on, eager to clear the next hurdle.

Though their stories are different and their backgrounds varied, each of these people is driven by something. Fear drives Andy Grove—fear of being overtaken or made obsolete by a competitor. Complacency is his great enemy.

For Fred Smith, the motivator is "Kaleidoscope thinking," the ability to take a business problem and turn it over and around enough times to see what may be a very nontraditional solution to it. Peter Lynch, a self-avowed workaholic, was propelled by the desire to create wealth for thousands of fund shareholders. Pleasant Rowland was pushed by a passion deep in her heart to provide little girls with a way to have fun and learn at the same time. Paul Volcker was driven to excel as a public servant by the example his crusading father set for him.

Other commonalities: extreme energy levels, monomaniacal focus, exacting methods, and organizational skills. Andy Grove answers all his electronic mail. Fred Smith spends four hours a day reading. Peter Lynch traveled to a supermarket and bought 50 pairs of pantyhose in order to research the company that made them. Pleasant Rowland makes decisions all the way down to which color of needlework one of her dolls should be working on. Paul Volcker stood up to two U.S. presidents in his efforts to do the right thing.

The humility found in these five folks may surprise you, particularly given the way the business press often transforms business successes into gods. Each one of them knows that life, even for those at the top of their game, is nothing if not humbling.

But the most common trait of all among these achievers is this: They are true believers, fanatics, zealots, people so convinced that their idea will win, that nothing can divert them from its implementation.

Five extraordinary people, five fascinating dialogues, five great minds. Let us introduce you.

CHAPTER ONE

ANDREW GROVE

CHAIRMAN,
CEO AND CO-FOUNDER,
INTEL CORPORATION

➤ ➤ ➤

ANDREW GROVE

CHAIRMAN,
CEO AND CO-FOUNDER,
INTEL CORPORATION

Andrew Grove, president and chief executive officer of Intel Corporation, is the quintessential American success story. Born in Budapest, Hungary, he left his homeland when he was just 20 years old. The year was 1956 and the Communist threat was becoming a dark reality across Eastern Europe. Grove emigrated to the United States of America penniless, knowing no English.

After teaching himself the language, Grove graduated from City College of New York in 1960 with a bachelor's degree in chemical engineering. He moved west to study at the University of California at Berkeley in 1963 where he earned his PhD. Sunny California agreed with him; he soon joined the research and development laboratory of Fairchild Semiconductor. In 1967, he became assistant director of R&D there.

It was at Fairchild that Grove met the inventor of the microprocessor and the man who would become his mentor—

Gordon Moore. In July 1968, Moore left Fairchild to start his own company. He lured Grove with him and together with Robert Noyce the three founded Intel Corporation. Less than ten years later, Grove was Intel's president. In 1987 he was named chief executive officer; in 1996 he rose to chairman.

Although Grove is now most famous as a superlative management strategist, he is also a respected inventor and teacher. He holds several patents on semiconductor devices and technology. He has taught graduate courses in semiconductor physics at U.C. Berkeley and currently lectures at Stanford's Graduate School of Business, in a course entitled "Strategy and Action in the Information Processing Industry."

A rigorous day job has not prevented Grove from writing four books. His first, *Physics and Technology of Semiconductor Devices* (John Wiley & Sons, 1967) has been used at leading universities in the United States. *High Output Management* (Random House, 1983) has been translated into 11 languages. *One-On-One with Andy Grove* (G.P. Putnam's Sons, 1987) and *Only the Paranoid Survive* (Doubleday, 1996) are his most recent efforts.

In 1995, Grove made public his ongoing battle with prostate cancer. His high-profile revelation was designed to bring attention to what is the fastest-growing disease among American men. Although his cancer is currently in remission, he is a major fund-raiser for cancer research into the disease and is out in front publicizing its dangers. He is married and has three daughters.

An intense man, Grove reveals that he is almost always afraid. He believes, however, that fear is not to be avoided as an enemy. Rather, it is an ally that business people should use to their advantage.

Grove learned the hard way that fear can help managers protect themselves from being blindsided by corporate crises, an inevitability of modern life. He speaks of crises from experience and knows well the power of denial. Indeed, perhaps the biggest battle that managers must fight is the one against what Grove calls *comfortable equilibrium,* the status quo. The only way you can win the battle against a false sense of ease and security is to make fear your friend.

Grove likens this to the way the human body uses physical pain as an ally. "It's fear that gets you out of comfortable equilibrium," he says. "That gets you to do the difficult tasks. I don't want to eliminate fear, whether it's fear of change or a fear of what's going to happen if you don't move. It's healthy, like physical pain is healthy. It warns your body that something is wrong. And just extinguishing pain doesn't make the problem go away."

What Andy Grove has learned from Intel's crises—what he calls *strategic inflection points*—is that wisdom means the difference between success on the business battlefield and abject failure. The difference between billions in profits and Chapter 11. The difference between industry dominance and defeat.

＞ ＞ ＞

Q: When you first joined Intel in 1968, did you foresee the impact that the silicon chip would have on the world's industry? Did you sort of see the future?

A: No. And not only did I not have a vision of the future, to tell you the truth, I didn't spend a minute thinking about it. The process of starting a company is not at all like that—at least, not for me. I was 32 years old, and what I was worrying about was getting a post office box so that when I sent out requests for information from manufacturers of equipment and material there was someplace for the information to get sent to. Then, of course, I was worried about whether we would be able to produce a product. So I was looking very much down at my toes for the next pebble that was going to trip us. So, no. My vision was only of one mundane thing after another.

Q: In hindsight, it looks like you knew exactly what you were doing, that you were consciously bringing this company to the place where it is now and to all that it has achieved now. But you're saying that it was really more like one step at a time?

A: It was one step at a time—and not all the steps were equal. Some were stutter steps, more or less stepping along the same direction. Others were kind of jumps to the side. But it was never a smooth process. Not then, not ten years later, and not now.

You cannot just evolve a business, responding to stimuli and the environment. You have to look back and analyze how you respond to things—that gives you a better perspective, a longer-range sense going forward. In fact, Bob Noyce—one of the founders of Intel—once said: 'An organization can look forward about as long as its history is going backwards.'

Q: Meaning that a company that's ten years old can only really look ahead a decade?

A: Yes. Noyce said that very early in the game at Intel when there was very little in the way of history. Later, there was a time when this statement could be applied and work reasonably well, but now that we have a 28-year history, I sure as hell can't fast-forward 28 years. So, I think we have passed the stage where that measure is really applicable.

Q: You talk about the stimuli that you as a manager must react to and something that is absolutely imperative for managers to see and react to is dramatic forces of change. The kind of change that, if you're ready for it, can take you to the next level, but that if you're unprepared for, can be your undoing. In fact, how you have managed change is an impressive part of your success and Intel's success. Yet change really intimidates people; it's very frightening. What do you think people—managers, just regular folks—can do to alleviate the scariness of change?

A: I'm not sure you want to eliminate scariness. I really wonder if tightrope walkers can do their job not because they are unafraid of heights, but because they are afraid of heights and they simply learn how to do their tasks that much better because of their fear. Because they know what it's like or they have a pretty good idea what it's like to fall.

I think fear is your ally in management because it's fear that gets you out of comfortable equilibrium—gets you to do the difficult tasks. You know, managing is not an easy job. Recently I had to do something that was very unpleasant. By necessity, it hurt somebody else's feelings. I was telling a colleague of mine,

'You know, we managers when we were little children must have enjoyed tearing wings off flies,' because constantly you have to do things that are painful either to someone else or to yourself. And you don't want to do those things. I mean, we are not people who really enjoy doing painful things. You do painful things because you fear that if you don't, something even worse is going to happen.

So, I don't want to eliminate fear. I don't want to eliminate fear of change. I don't want to eliminate the fear of what's going to happen if you don't move. Fear is healthy. In the same way that physical pain is healthy, because it warns your body that something is wrong. And just extinguishing pain doesn't make the problem go away. It just makes your sense that there is a problem go away. So you're in an even worse predicament.

Q: But one of the problems with fear is the natural reaction to it, the denial which often accompanies fear. Since denial is a normal reaction to fear, how do you get around that?

A: What you need to do is train people that the way to respond to fear is by moving, by going forward, by taking charge of your destiny. That's much preferable to the alternative: being paralyzed, pretending that the problem causing your anxiety isn't there. But you have to accept that people will be afraid. Don't try to pretend that they shouldn't be.

Q: Easier said than done.

A: Of course. A good manager will try to train people how to deal with fear by example, by discussion, by cognitive processes. Lead employees to react in an active fashion to that fear. Encourage them to accept that when something happens in the environment, it's up to all of us to take control of our destiny. You have to put their minds in gear to figure out what to do about the problem and to throw themselves into whatever the new course of action is. That is trainable, particularly if the leader of an organization becomes a role model for this type of action.

Q: Did you train yourself how to do that? Was it something that you had learned over long periods? Or was there a pivotal event in which you learned how to deal with fear?

A: I think it's something you learn over a long period of time, but at the same time there are certain events which are exceptional that etch themselves in your memory. One of those was in 1985 when Gordon Moore—our chairman—and I were discussing what to do about our deteriorating business in computer memory chips.

Q: Intel had been very big in memory chips, correct? Wasn't this your bread-and-butter business?

A: Correct. But over a period of time we had lost a large portion of our market share to Japanese producers. We were bleeding money and we'd gone through all the rationalization and the denial and the management-by-hope that people do to try to get out of a bind. And nothing worked.

So Gordon and I were talking about various things—what we could do, what we should do—and they were all in the context of the current approach to things, the current strategy, the current business model, which was as a very big player in the memory business.

And I said to Gordon: 'What would happen if the board kicked us out and hired a bunch of new people? What would they do?' Without a moment's hesitation Gordon said, 'They would get us out of the memory business.'

Q: Even though this was what had brought Intel to the heights of success and profitability, indeed what had made Intel a brand name in chips?

A: That's right. But by the time I'm describing, the business had turned sour on us. Even so, it was very difficult for us to contemplate as a rational option that we would get out of that business, precisely because we had created that business in the first place.

But when a problem is articulated in the form 'What would somebody else do?,' it was a lot easier to come up with that option than when we were merely asking what should we do about the problem. And then, of course, the question was: 'Well, why don't we go out the revolving door and come back as if we were somebody they just hired and do it ourselves?' And that was an important moment for me because that's exactly what we did. And it worked out well over time.

I often use that mental model in lesser situations, asking myself what would somebody without the emotional ties to the problem do? It doesn't always work—it's like a mental gimmick with which you prepare yourself to face something difficult. When it works, you get more actual answers than the answer you get sitting where you are, immersed in the product of your experiences. You try to remove yourself from it to force yourself to be more objective.

Q: You have said that as a manager, you are concerned about having the outsider's perspective, bringing the outsider's perspective to your business. This is extremely difficult to do, it's so easy to be insulated. How do you do that?

A: Well, there are two aspects to that. One is how do you do it so that you are exposed to the stimuli from the outside perspective? And then second, how do you do it emotionally? What we've been talking about—let's go out the revolving door and come back and pretend we're somebody else—that is how you trick yourself, if you succeed, to act like an outsider emotionally.

But even before you do that, you have to see yourself and see your world with the experiences of an outsider. That you can get by mixing with outsiders. You can isolate yourself and run your business basically just talking to inside people who will tell you what the outside world tells them, or you can mix and match and spend a fair amount of time with people who sell to you and therefore work very hard to convince you of their point of view.

Or you can talk to people you sell to who are—particularly when unhappy—very vocal about what's wrong with what you're doing. You can go to trade shows and look at competitors' products and look at customers' products. You can read.

There's a lot of ways that you can expose yourself to the outside world, but you have to take a certain amount of initiative. And when you do that and when the people inside your organization bring you assessments and evaluations of the outside world so that you are no longer isolating yourself, their tendency to sugarcoat their information is going to be minimized. After all, they know that you've got independent news of your own, that you're getting a reality check on their information.

So, it works altogether that their information—which you get through inside means—will be more realistic and also more helpful.

Q: The happy ending to this story, of course, is that you turned Intel's troubles into an opportunity. You turned the company around, going from losing money to profitability, in two years. That's a pretty phenomenal turnaround time. For a company that had to go through such a profound change, exiting a business that was its lifeblood.

A: We took some pretty dramatic action. We cut the size of the company back by about one-third in terms of people in a matter of months. In terms of facilities—we shut down eight locations, about a third of what we had then. Once we accepted that we have to do these things, we did them in a characteristically Intel way: goal-oriented, output-oriented, systematic method. Once we decided that that's what we had to do, we executed our strategy pretty effectively.

And, fortunately, we did it at the right time. The microprocessor business did come back and it came back in the United States. The personal computer business reemerged as a strong driving force for our business. So, things went well for us. The strategy was right and we focused on microprocessors and it worked.

Q: Are you fairly confident that such a massive problem will not come out of left field again? The Japanese situation didn't exactly come out of left field, but it wreaked havoc on an entire industry.

A: It came out of left field in terms of magnitude: absolutely without parallel in our industry. Had we really studied other industries, we wouldn't have been as surprised because ten years earlier the Japanese wiped out the U.S.-based consumer electronics industry just as fast and just as dramatically. But we were only vaguely aware of that. It was another industry and we didn't make the association.

But am I comfortable that something like this couldn't happen? No. I don't think I'm comfortable. I live in fear. And I have no intention of lulling myself into comfort. I worry about what such a thing could be. I worry about a bunch of things that happen or a bunch of things that don't happen. What's even more insidious is when something goes out of the market— something goes out of the technology. The vitality gradually disappears, so it's not even something that somebody else does to you. But suppose your technology or your business idea loses its allure, or loses its zip or its energy. That's even more subtle. So,

I worry about those things and I hope a lot of people at Intel worry about it along with me, because it's not one person's worry.

Q: Is that your biggest concern, now? That the computer business will lose its zip?

A: My biggest concern is: this is a very big business. It's a worldwide business and it's a business with a phenomenal track record of the last ten years. It grew very rapidly and transformed; the product constantly got reinvented every couple of years. And this formula works. The product gets better. It finds new customers and new uses. It has worked very well. God didn't create the formula. A lot of hard work went into reinventing the PC in the right way—finding new uses for it, finding new users for it, finding them wherever in the world.

I worry about maintaining the engine of reinvention, of new customers and new uses and keeping that engine going. It is by no means preordained that it was to have happened in the past or that it is going to happen in the future. So, it deserves worry.

Q: Indeed, the personal computer has transformed itself from just a box on a desk that you can either work or play games on into a communications tool. And that, of course, is what the Internet brings to this business and all of the attendant hopes and, as you say, fears about it.

How are you going to make sure that that PC becomes the worldwide communication tool that it has the promise to be?

A: Fortunately, we are actually a little bit ahead of the curve on this one because we started to surmise that communication was going to be the new use for the personal computer some years ago. So, what we started to do then was amass the internal capability required to understand the technology involved with communications, to understand what we need to do to our microprocessors and to the PC platform itself to make it do a good job in communications. Data coming into the computer, for example, has to be considered. Specifically, how you process those data so that it is synergistic with the communication process.

Then you have to ask what kind of data will make it appealing for people to use a computer as a communication device. And all you have to do is look around the radio and television and say is it going to be that kind of data? It's bound to involve sound; it's bound to involve video. Now what do you have to do to modify the platform? What do you have to do to modify the microprocessors? So you start thinking along this line and bringing people who have contributions to make, who have expertise in the area. And you keep it going.

The significance of the Internet in all that is that, without the Internet, this would have been a very, very slow process. To bring effective flow of data from computer to computer is an enormous undertaking, requiring huge amounts of money. And the Internet enabled a lot of the existing communication networks to be adapted and used for that purpose. This is wonderful because the PC's utility as a communication device is strictly proportional to the ability of the connection infrastructure to deliver data. All of a sudden, because of the Internet it's rapidly available. So, right now we are working double time to make use of all that data that's coming on the Internet or that can come on the Internet. Store it, manipulate it, create it, collate it, and make it easier for the user to do whatever he or she wants to do. So now it's pretty easy to see what we need to do for the next two or three years. And beyond that, of course, I have no idea.

Q: Would you equate the personal computer with other revolutionary objects in business history, say, Henry Ford's assembly line or Edison's lightbulb? Or do you think it's something different?

A: It's very difficult for me to answer that question because I wasn't around when those things happened; I only read about them in history books. The development of the PC is something I lived through day by day, pebble by pebble, step by step. In my view it came slowly, gradually, a bit at a time.

It is entirely possible that if you ask this question of somebody who was not in the personal computer industry ten to twenty years ago, the PC may look as revolutionary as the light bulb. But being an internal participant, it doesn't look similar to me at all. It looked like a very gradual thing. I remember every little skirmish in it.

Q: One of the things that I see as a business writer is that all areas of business seem to be speeding up. Innovations do not last as long or throw off the years of profitability that they used to. The churn of change seems so much more dramatic and fast. Why is this? What do you attribute this to?

A: Well, first of all, let me say you are right. It used to be when we had a good idea we could take advantage of it for some period of time. Now we find we have a good idea, particularly in the general area of Internet connectivity and things of that sort, three months later we find that there are six start-up companies doing the exact same thing. And some are behind us and some are ahead of us, but the difference between behind us and ahead of us is measured in a few months. So it is comparable to the first few years of personal computing, but then the personal computer was a contained little niche area of activity in terms of the spectrum of things in the world. Now, Internet and personal computing are everywhere in the world.

So, this fervor and churning affects everything. I think three things cause it. Number one, the computer industry has become so big and so pervasive that it just draws not thousands of people into the group of interested parties, but millions. So you've got the intellectual energy, curiosity, creative contributions of millions of people doing this. That's point one.

Second, the stakes are so enormous that you've got all kinds of money available for this. Billions of dollars go into this, the same billions of dollars that can't find their way to build communications infrastructure, automatically go into computer-related venture capital. So, there's a lot of money and a lot of smart, driven people involved.

The third reason is kind of funny: The tools of the connected personal computer are being used to propagate knowledge, information, news of these inventions and discoveries, propositions from one place to the other, all at the speed of light. So the medium of interconnected personal computers is being used to speed the process of improving that medium. So, it is kind of a feedback system.

Q: And it's all your fault.

A: It's all our fault. That's right, part of it anyway.

Q: But it must make your life a challenge as it does every business person's everywhere.

A: Yes. It also makes it very interesting. Every day in the midafternoon, I check up with one of my on-line news services to see what happened today and almost every day there is some news that goes on that I find surprising and important. Not colossal, but important. Important enough, for instance, that I want to tell somebody about it. Every time I pick up a business newspaper there's something in there that surprises me from someplace. So it's a very interesting world, ours.

Q: And you don't see it slowing down any time soon?

A: No, I don't think so.

Q: One of the interesting changes in the personal computer business is the move away from vertical integration—where a personal computing company such as Apple built its computers from the ground up, the operating system, the box, everything. Today that manufacturing style has been replaced by a horizontal one, where a number of different companies—one making the operating system, another making the chips—contribute to the end result. Do you see this happening in other areas of business as well?

A: It is happening everywhere. My knowledge of other industries, of course, is much more superficial; it's a distant observer's knowledge, but consider the automobile business. It used to be when one of these Ford plants were built, you know, tree logs would come in one gate, rubber would come in another gate, or iron ore would come in another building and cars would roll out the other end. Today car manufacturers swap engines—sometimes maybe too easily. There are independent manufacturers—electronic subsystems for cars. Obviously, tires have long been produced by suppliers to the automotive industry. So, the vertical integration that existed 50 years ago is history in the car industry.

Then there's transportation. Some years ago the trend was to combine car rentals with the airline industry and hotel industry. But none of those combinations worked. There are pretty fundamental economic forces driving industries toward a horizontal model when they become big and when they become fast-paced. And people do try to verticalize—a terrible verb—some industries.

Everyone says, 'Wow!' But I can't think of a single successful attempt at that recently—and recently I mean the last ten years. So, I think the trends are pretty strongly toward a universal, horizontal arrangement of businesses. Another way to look at it—toward specialization, which is also another way to say that the more competitive the industry is, the more narrowly you have to specialize in order to keep up with other specialists. If you are vertical, by necessity you are trying to master several elements of your product or your service. You can't possibly be equally good at all of those things.

Q: Andy, why did you first join Intel? Did you see something about the company, where it could go in the future that made you think this was the place to be?

A: There are two answers. Technologically and businesswise I saw one thing. But the main reason was that I really liked working with Gordon Moore, and when Gordon said he is going to go off and do this thing, I barely knew and cared very little what it was going to be. I was just going to go with Gordon. I hesitate to put it this way but it was that simple.

But I did also think about what this might mean technologically, and to understand my answer you have to go back a little bit in time. Computer memory originally was built out of little doughnut-like magnetic cores—tiny little ones—that people strung on wires manually. It was very labor-intensive, lots and lots of production workers would go and manually string wires through those little magnetic cores. What Intel's technology offered to do was replace those things in the form of lots of transistors that are all fabricated using semiconductor technology—lots of them at the same time.

So, technologically, we could string those memory devices together—thousands at a time, later on hundreds of thousands, later on millions at a time—eliminating the need for manually doing this. So this obviously had the advantage of achieving productivity through technology. When it was all just beginning, it seemed very promising, and, in fact, it happened very much along those lines.

So, yes, I understood there was a real basis for doing this. But the real driving force is I was just going to go with Gordon.

Q: One of the biggest contributions that you've made at Intel is to make the public aware of your product's importance inside a computer. This is the 'Intel Inside' advertising campaign, which is designed to make the consumer, who normally wouldn't care what microprocessor was inside his computer, want to buy a machine with an Intel chip inside. Effectively, you turned something from a commodity into a branded item consumers would shop for.

When did you first come up with this ad campaign? There are risks to the strategy as well as rewards. How did you analyze the risk/reward in this?

A: Well, it was kind of obvious in a way. If you listened to the language people used to describe the computer at the time— we're talking late 1980s—most people would refer to their computer by the number of the microprocessors inside the machine. They would say: 'I'm going to take my trusty old 386 and do something on it.'

They didn't use the name of the manufacturer, they used the model number of the microprocessor, which actually is kind of right. Because the fundamental characteristic of the computer is the microprocessor. That defines what software it's going to run, how fast it will run it, and what you can do with it. So the user experience—what the user can do and how well he or she can do it, more than anything else depends on the microprocessor, the chip.

So, we sensed that we really already had that identity. We didn't know exactly how to go about it. We wanted to market the product name, but the problem with the product name was we couldn't copyright it—we couldn't trademark the numbers. We had a legal battle on it and lost. So, how do we tell our story? Given that the microprocessor, more than anything else, gives the characteristic of the computer to the user, and we started merchandising, 'Intel, the computer inside.' Not on the devices, but in our own commercials. And that kind of worked. We had good focus group results. People understood, 'Yeah, the Intel stuff is the computer inside.'

So it came in steps, like so many things. We didn't have a precise plan on what we were going to do and how we were going to do it. But it was driven by an understanding that the fundamental truth, namely that the characteristic of the computer is more than anything else defined by the microprocessor. And that was accepted by the end users. So that's how it happened.

Q: So, how much now do you think Intel's success is marketing and how much of it is technology?

A: You know, for a long time I've thought about this and I have to answer the question internally a lot. The best I can do is describe Intel as a three-legged stool. And the three legs are design, technology and manufacturing, and marketing and sales. And if one of those legs is shorter than the other, the stool will tip over. I mean, if they're not equally strong or one is shorter than the other, the stool will tip over.

I think that has been true for a long time, but the nature of the design lag and the nature of the technology and manufacturing lag, and the nature of the sales and marketing lag change in the process. But the need to keep the three of them in balance has remained constant for ten to fifteen years. It just means different things today. Today marketing means communicating messages to millions of people, not to thousands of other companies' engineers. So it means something different, but it has about a one-third kind of role.

Q: Speaking of marketing, another crisis point in Intel's recent past involved the Pentium chip, when you found a very slight problem with the chip's mathematical capabilities. What was your reaction to that problem? Could you discuss what happened and describe what you went through in that experience?

A: The Pentium chip problem was a dramatic way for us at Intel to learn that we were truly dealing with the millions of consumers rather than hundreds of engineers. Because of the

'Intel Inside' ad campaign, we decided to advertise our micro-processors to consumers. Sometimes you make one part of a change, one part of an adaptation and not another. And I think that was the case here. We were used to doing our marketing communications from engineer to engineer—talking very technical language. Then we started merchandising our micro-processors to millions of consumers without really realizing that consumer marketing is much more simplified and much more impressionistic. You don't have the time and space or the capability to get into rational, technical arguments.

So we had this problem: We were dealing with unnamed millions of consumers and trying to reason with them as if we were sitting across a conference table from a bunch of engineers. And it didn't work. So, that was a very sobering learning experience that we figured out that our support systems have to adapt to our marketing messages. If you market to the consumer, you have to support the consumer.

Q: How long did that take you to figure out?

A: Oh, it didn't take long in calendar time. It took years out of our lives. It was a very painful experience.

Q: But ultimately, the Pentium chips are now fine and there's very little residual ill will.

A: Well, the technical issue was fixed very quickly. Dealing with the consumer took longer. Learning how to deal with them on their terms. But we learned that too. Actually, in retrospect, the whole thing was just a few weeks, but it seemed similar to the memory chip crisis which went on for years.

Q: One of the aspects of your management style is to do post-mortems regularly, to analyze every success and every failure that the company has. What does that do for you? Is such an analytical process common in American business today?

A: Analyzing success is not truly necessary. Success has many, many fathers, and success gets told many, many times. So, that's not too necessary. There is a tendency, however, to walk away from failure and leave it buried. And there's an enormous amount of institutional learning that gets lost because failures don't get analyzed. So, the real learning is in actual fact what is learned from failure, because something wasn't done or something was done wrong, something didn't work. And unless you address those things they will not be done or they will not work in the future. So, the real improvement of the organization or an improvement in its capabilities or products comes from analyzing failures.

The reason people don't do this is because there is an altogether too large a tendency, I would say probably in our society, but certainly at Intel, to assign blame to groups, organizations, or individuals. It didn't work because you didn't do X. Well, it didn't work because those turkeys in manufacturing botched it up, or something like that. That doesn't teach you anything.

You've got to go way below that and discipline yourself. The purpose of this learning is not to assign blame, but to learn exactly what went wrong in a rational, objective fashion. The purpose of this exercise is to make the process or the product better, not to assign blame.

It's not easy to keep that discipline, but it's very useful. So we try to do that.

Q: The title of your most recent book is *Only the Paranoid Survive,* which is apparently one of the comments that you're famous for.

What are other characteristics besides paranoia and fear as you describe it that make for a successful CEO today? And have those characteristics changed dramatically, would you say, in the last 20, 50, or 100 years?

A: I think one critical element that an earlier book of mine tried to capture in its title—it was called *High Output Management*—is keeping your eye on the output. You're doing things for a purpose. You're doing things because you want to achieve a result and putting the result constantly in front of your eyes will keep you on track much better than when you don't.

The alternative is, you can get caught up in the process of things, get caught up in the appearance of things, get caught up in the trappings and forget what output you wanted, the result you wanted in the first place. I think, again, like every other conduct, this type of focus gets propagated in an organization by the leadership of that organization role modeling it. So, it's very important for the heads of organizations to be focused on results—measuring results, rewarding results and not conduct and behavior and styles and all these other things that have at best a tenuous and speculative link to results. I would nominate that as the other item.

Your second question is have these things changed? I really don't know. My suspicion is that they probably haven't. When you read Shakespeare and look at what leadership meant in the time of Richard III, it doesn't sound altogether different from what it means today. And if the elements of leadership didn't change in 500 years, why would they have changed in the last 20 or 30?

Q: The whole concept of change and how much change is rocking your industry and the entire world and how much faster change has taken place brings me to a question. There's one area that seems impervious to the massive change we've been discussing, and that is the government. It seems to be so insulated inside the Beltway that it appears almost impregnable. Do you agree? And, if so, when will this situation change?

A: Well, I don't agree. I think we can look at this a little differently if you include not just our government but a number of other governments in the world. The government of the Soviet Union was impervious to change and impervious to change and impervious to change, and all of a sudden when the forces acting on it became big enough, not only is the government gone, the Soviet Union is gone. So, there's plenty of examples of forces in the world becoming powerful enough to take otherwise untouchable governments and turn them upside down.

Now, what is actually remarkable about the American system is this: Because of constant elections, where people get thrown out and people resign, it is capable of incremental change. So, it really is changing constantly; this means you can avoid the cataclysmic upheaval that those governments that are not capable of changing incrementally have to endure. So, I think we are seeing change.

Q: Well, that's encouraging.

A: The discouraging part about it is it is not speeding up. You know, everything in business has sped up a whole lot more, so while I give credit for our government's ability to change, it's very slow. Inasmuch as American business became world-competitive over a period of time in the 1980s—which was very tough on all of us—that kind of monumental change is not present in government. So the good news about our system is it's capable of incremental change. The bad news is that it's only capable of incremental change.

Q: Interesting. You bring up the American place in the world of business. What do you see as the future for American companies in the global marketplace? Do we have, as Americans, any characteristics that make us better able to compete or less able to compete?

A: To generalize, I think we have regained the ability to compete in world business reasonably well by changing our attitude. It comes from perhaps the 1950s when American business was so predominant that we were very self-righteous and convinced that our way was by far the best way. That got us into the turmoil of the 1970s and the 1980s when a lot of companies came out a lot more humbled, a lot more pragmatic. Then we were able to accept the role of one of the key economic powers but not the predominant economic power.

As we accepted that reality, we became a lot more competitive. So, I would classify us as a vital economic power, certainly one of the leading economic powers and trading partners. We are one of the leading sources of technology, but by no means the source of technology. That adjustment was the story of the 1980s.

Q: So we don't have the inertia of success working against us?

A: No. Correct. We paid our dues for that inertia of success in a pretty tough ten-to-fifteen-year period.

Q: Is it true that you read all of your e-mail, both internal and external? How do you find time to do this? And what does it bring you?

A: It helps bring information and perspectives without filters. It also helps me to respond to things very quickly. I can exchange messages two or three times a day on a subject or issue and resolve relatively complex matters between people that may be in three different continents at a given time. E-mail gives immediacy to issues. It's like the difference between driving a car with mittens on or driving cars with your fingers on the steering wheel. You feel the bumps of the road this way. It takes time, but it also replaces time. I mean, I spend probably an hour and a half, two hours a day on e-mail, but I used to spend an hour and a half, two hours a day reading paper mail and that has almost disappeared.

Q: Is this going to change the way business is done, do you think?

A: Absolutely. It speeds everything up, as we talked about it. I don't know how we could conduct business today without it. The most vital business system at Intel today in terms of computers and communications is our e-mail system. It is more important than the telephone. Far more important.

Q: Do you think there will ever be a point when you're taken by surprise again by some aspect of your business?

A: Well, the point of living in fear is to avoid being taken by surprise. So, if my fear leads to constructive action, the answer to that is no. If I release that tension or let the tension go away, or if I make a mistake, then yes it can happen. There's no guarantee against that.

Q: But you're ever vigilant?

A: I try to be. I hope I am. You never know. It's only after the fact that you could know. 'Hey, I was on the ball and I avoided this one. Or I took advantage of that opportunity.' But you never can see in advance.

Q: Intel expends a ton of money on research and development. What are you investing in right now that you believe could be the next big thing?

A: I don't think I can identify the next big thing. We are working on so many different elements of the next generations of microprocessors, which involve architecture, silicon technology, design techniques, different wafer sizes, manufacturing techniques, even software to take advantage of what we build into the microprocessors. It's a very broad set of activities, all of which give us another generation of computing capabilities—us and the world.

But most of our effort continues to be focused on our core business, which is computing and communications and making it better and faster and making it do more things than computers did before.

Q: You were an immigrant to this nation and you have achieved more than the American dream. I wonder if there is anything in your experience as a newcomer to this country that prepared you for your success at Intel or that drove it in some way?

A: A lot of people have tried to find something in my background that would necessitate it, and I can't. I mean, I've lived the life I had. I had to be energetic throughout life, but I'm not unique in that. Most people who emigrated at a relatively early age—for that matter any age—had to be pretty energetic to adjust to a new society, a new language, a new way of doing things. You have to be somewhat energetic typically to leave a previous life behind; some of them have done well and some of them have not done so well. So, being an immigrant does not guarantee success in America or anywhere else.

Q: Where do you think Intel would be if Andy Grove had never come along? If you had gone somewhere else?

A: I've not thought about it that way, but I've thought about where I would be had I not gone to Intel.

Q: Well, that's a good one too. We'll take that, as well.

A: Well, Intel has been very good to me and I think I probably would have done okay elsewhere, too, but I had such coincidence of breaks here, you know, working for someone like Gordon who encouraged me to change and expand and supported me, even now.

I started to work for Gordon when I got out of graduate school, coming to work for him at Fairchild Semiconductor and at Intel and he's been my mentor as we both changed through life. That's a very fortunate occurrence, and it's not so much to do with Intel, it's a somewhat personal situation. I hope that I made my corresponding contribution to that. And I think I carried my weight in 28 years at Intel, but I know that Intel carried its weight in allowing me and encouraging me to develop in a pretty effective way. But it's been a good relationship.

I like what I do and I like who I do it with. And that gets the best part of anyone.

Q: Your career has been tremendously enriching to you, it's been enriching to Intel's shareholders and to the nation's PC users. Do you think you will be the last to know, as you say in your book, when it comes time for you to move on? Or is that one of the things that you're going to be ever vigilant about?

A: That's a subject I think a lot about and I actually have thought a lot about before because I see examples around me of people in the industry or people in other industries who have stayed around too long. And I'd prefer to move on at a time when the reaction to people is, 'Why?' As compared to, 'It's about time.' So, on the one hand that is one factor. On the other hand, I like what I'm doing. And so the right answer to this would be to err on the side of too early rather than too late. Heaven only knows if I have the objectivity and the self-discipline to do that, but that's my aim.

CHAPTER TWO

FRED SMITH

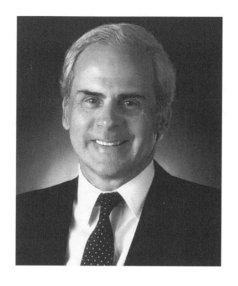

FOUNDER AND CEO,
FEDERAL EXPRESS
CORPORATION

❯ ❯ ❯

FRED SMITH

FOUNDER AND CEO,
FEDERAL EXPRESS
CORPORATION

It is not quite accurate to say that Frederick W. Smith built a multibillion dollar industry from scratch. Yes, he created the express delivery business which now generates more than $20 billion in annual revenues. But there's more to it. In creating the industry, he helped make the creaky U.S. Postal Service more responsive to its customers. He has also supported thousands of small technology companies by buying their goods. And, with his company's superlative service record, he's helped countless companies perform in their own marketplaces that much better. Truly Fred Smith's creation of Federal Express has touched millions of lives.

But Smith has another accomplishment to add to these. He is that rarity: an entrepreneur who has made the often wrenching transition to manager. Smith has proven himself equally adept at dreaming up an industry and then managing it, day-to-day.

Frederick Wallace Smith was born August 11, 1944, near Memphis, Tennessee, the son of a flamboyant Southern business-man who made a fortune running a bus service and restaurants during the Depression. Smith went north to school, attending Yale University where, in 1965, he wrote an economics term paper proposing the concept that would later become Federal Express. Believing that the U.S. economy was becoming more technology-driven, Smith held that there would soon be a mar-ket for overnight, door-to-door delivery of packages or docu-ments. How far ahead of his time was Smith? *So far* that his economics professor gave the undergraduate a "C" on the paper.

In 1966, Smith was graduated with a B.A. in economics and political science. He served two tours of duty as a Marine in Vietnam, receiving the Silver Star, a Bronze Star, and two Pur-ple Hearts. On one occasion, a Viet Cong bullet blew away his helmet's chin strap, but he was unhurt.

Smith's war experience still resonates, even today. But back then it drove him to start something. "I got so sick of destruc-tion that I came back determined to do something construc-tive," he once recalled.

It took him several years to convince investors that his idea for an overnight, reasonably priced delivery system could fly. But in March 1973, Federal Express flew its first flight. Smith had amassed an amazing $42 million from investors, bankers, and family members, making FedEx the largest start-up funded by venture capital at that time. FedEx began serving 25 cities and its first shipment totaled 186 packages. Today, 2 million pounds of packages fly through FedEx's Memphis sorting ware-house on a given night.

But FedEx's success was not immediate. As Smith points out, "Any paradigmatic shift is very hard [to sell] because you're going against the conventional wisdom." He recalls his own task in selling Federal Express. "The problem about FedEx is that it was a network. You can't sell a network before a network exists. So there was a huge amount of front-loading in terms of capital and assets to be able to offer a network that we could sell."

Planes, trucks, warehouses, offices. All had to be in place, up and ready to run before Smith could sell his concept to American business. A staggering challenge.

A personal trait that kept Smith going throughout the greatest challenges was his ability to maintain a sense of humor and humility. He may command 500 planes, 36,000 trucks, and 120,000 employees, but he never took it all too seriously. His experiences building FedEx were always kept in perspective.

"Remember, I had been in the Marine Corps in Vietnam," Smith says. "So what we were really talking about was money, not life and death issues. Had I not had that perspective, I would have been much more emotionally flattened by the difficulties of putting the company together. But once having started it and gone down the road, you're a little bit crazy and you're driven towards the end goal and that provides a lot of adrenaline."

Interestingly, Smith says he never really had a role model after which he patterned himself or his company. Nor did he have an interest in getting rich off his idea. Rather, he saw a way he could revolutionize the way business operated.

How hard is it to make the transition from entrepreneur to manager? Are the two personality types mutually exclusive?

Smith thinks not. But he does concede that the energy required to keep an organization going makes day-to-day management harder than many entrepreneurs realize. "A lot of people think, 'Well, I can be looking ahead and have somebody else worrying about those day-to-day things.' But it doesn't really work that cleanly," Smith says. Nevertheless, it's crucial for the success of the organization that the inventor be allowed to keep inventing.

Looking ahead, something he excels at, Smith sees profound change in several different business sectors in the following discussion. And, given his record as a visionary, one had best read on.

Fred Smith lives with his second wife Diane in Memphis, Tennessee. He has nine children.

➤ ➤ ➤

Q: Success as an entrepreneur depends upon the big idea—getting the big idea and implementing it. How did you come up with the idea that was going to create Federal Express, which really changed the way American business is done?

A: I suppose that the original idea for FedEx can be traced all the way back to the mid-sixties to an economics paper I did in college that looked at the changes that the computer was going to have on the business landscape. And I concluded that the logistics system that had served traditional industry would not work for a computerized society. And by that I mean traditional distribution systems were built on multilayered local and regional infrastructures.

The problem with that type of an infrastructure for people who were building computers was that their efficacy in the marketplace depended on the device they were selling working all the time. So, if IBM wanted to sell a computer to a banker in

Texas, it didn't make any difference to the banker that IBM had built the computer in Armonk, New York. The computer had to work every day if they were going to get rid of the clerks and substitute the computer to post the checks and so forth.

So, a company like IBM, as an example, had to have a logistics system that provided the parts and pieces wherever that computer was located whenever it was needed, and there was no ability to bring in a couple of temporaries or glue something together if it didn't work. And that was the original idea for FedEx. We would be the transportation system that an organization like IBM needed.

Later on, the methodology that was developed to service those logistic needs—the hub and spokes and the integrated air/ground system—was developed. But the original idea was you had to have a nondiscriminatory logistics system so that the parts and pieces that the computerized world needed would be available every day wherever they needed to be used to satisfy a customer.

Q: I see. And was this the famous term paper that did not earn you an 'A'?

A: Well, that's a little bit of an apocryphal story. It got exaggerated, but I'm smart enough to know it was turned into a great story. Everybody loves to flaunt authority and I answered the question one day, 'What did you get on that paper?' And I said, 'Well I don't really remember. I guess it was my usual gentlemanly "C." ' And that has now become part of the FedEx story.

Q: Well, let's assume it's more fact than fiction. Obviously the professor didn't see what you had seen, and that's very much part of being an entrepreneur. How did you see whatever it was you saw before anyone else did?

A: Well, I think if you look at the history of most entrepreneurial ideas, there's that common denominator that somebody had a different perspective or slightly different view of something than the traditional wisdom or the traditional thinking was at the time. That's a very common thing.

Q: Can that view or perspective be learned or can it be taught? Or is this something you think you're born with?

A: I think there's a lot of luck and I think it's probably intuition that's mostly there to begin with. I do think that you can teach people to think in those channels, however. One of my favorite terms is 'Kaleidoscope Thinking,' which I believe was coined by the former editor of the *Harvard Business Review,* Rosabeth Moss Kanter, and what she was trying to get across with that phrase is if you have a business problem and you turn the kaleidoscope and you mull it over, then sometimes perhaps you'll see it in a slightly different form than you had seen it traditionally.

So, I think you can get it across to people that there may be some different approaches if you'll just keep thinking about the business problem. That I think you can learn. And whether you're interested in doing it, that's something else.

Q: So you have to keep thinking of it, keep analyzing it in different ways, using as much information as you can. One of the ways that you get this information, I understand, is that you read four hours a day. How is it possible for you to take four hours out of your day running a giant corporation like FedEx? And what do you read?

A: I don't read very much fiction. Every once in a while I do. I mean, I'll be up at two o'clock in the morning reading a murder mystery. But I read a lot of history. I read a lot of business books, a lot of books on management. And I enjoy reading. It's my hobby. It's not as if I feel compelled to read. It's something I like to do. I'd much rather read a book than watch television.

Q: What in your reading has been most influential to you? Anything come to mind that really helped you?

A: I don't know that there's a single book. There's a body of management literature that I think is sort of a fundamental library that you have to have. If you're interested in management, you go back historically and read Henri Fayol and Frederick W. Taylor and, of course, you've got to understand what Peter Drucker said and Michael Porter. More recently Robert Waterman, Tom Peters, and Michael Hammer. There are not very many really important business books. And I think that the little library I just recounted gives anybody who wants to read those things a pretty solid foundation about business thinking.

I think what has been much more important to me are stories about people looking at things differently and creating an opportunity. One of my favorite stories is about Dr. Hans Selye, a Nobel laureate who developed most of the theory of trauma that modern medicine uses.

He used to tell a story about himself that when he was a young research assistant, I think up at the University of Rochester, he had been engaged in an experiment and one day he got his cultures and he looked at them and they were totally eaten up with green mold. And it was a year of his life down the drain in this experiment. And, of course, what he was looking at was penicillin.

And a doctor in England, named Alexander Fleming, was able to look at what Selye had seen and what traditionally was a very unwelcome thing to doctors—you know, mold and dirt—and see its life-saving properties. So Fleming invented penicillin and changed the world. He just looked at the problem slightly differently than Hans Selye.

Q: So, you had this view—this macroview of the business. How did you then build Federal Express into the ubiquitous company that it is today?

A: Well, FedEx was built on the original premise that the large, computerized society that was beginning to evolve would require a different logistics system. The methodology that I selected later to solve this business problem was in essence a gargantuan bank clearinghouse or a telecommunication switch.

Traditionally, transportation had been conducted on point-to-point routes. So, I would fly or put a truck or a railroad between point A and point B. The business problem that was presented by the Computer Age was much more akin to the telecommunications problem in that I had to connect a lot of different points all to one another at the same time. And the way to do that, of course, is to put a central switch or a clearinghouse in the case of a bank and rather than putting links between each point on the system, you just connect them through the central junction box.

That appears to be very inefficient if you take a transaction in isolation: the movement of an item from, say, Detroit to Minneapolis all the way through a central hub in Memphis. But when you take all of the transactions on the network together, it's tremendously efficient. And up to that point nobody had really applied that as comprehensively as we did. I mean, certainly, I didn't invent the concept. The post office in India used it. Delta Airlines used it. But applying it to the world of logistics was unique.

The other thing that I understood, which was a little bit of my background from the service, was that the same company could operate both trucks and planes. Historically those had been different corporate structures.

So, it was the adoption of that nationwide clearinghouse and an integrated air/ground system that allowed us to go to people and say, 'Look, if you have these parts and pieces that you need to supply from any point on this system, we can supply it to any of your customers overnight.' And there were a lot of other things that we had to do—raising the money, for instance. Breaking down all kinds of government barriers in order for us to operate our company the way customers wanted us to operate it, rather than in accordance with some sort of bureaucratic or regulatory regime. But it was that fundamental understanding of the market and that different approach to satisfying the market that led FedEx to become what now is an 11 billion dollar company.

Q: And a household name. Was it a hard sell?

A: Oh, sure. Absolutely. I think any paradigmatic shift is very hard because you're going against the conventional wisdom. And the other problem about FedEx is that it was a network. And obviously you can't sell a network before a network exists. It's very difficult to go in and say, 'I have wonderful telephone service between New York and Chicago.' And people are going to say, 'Well, come back when you can serve most of the other points in this country or around the world.'

So there was a huge amount of front-loading in terms of capital and assets to be able to offer a network that we could sell.

Q: There must have been many obstacles and hurdles. Raising the capital was probably difficult. But when you think back now, was there one turning point or one obstacle to overcome?

A: I think the biggest single thing that we did in the early days that served us well was the verification of customer demand through not one, not two, but three total independent marketing surveys. There was no question because of the research we did that there was a tremendous need that had to be satiated by some system.

Q: So this was before you'd raised the capital?

A: Yes. So we had the documented evidence that the market-place existed. And that's very different from some products or services which you have to manufacture before anybody can even conceive of them. But we were able to demonstrate that there was a significant requirement and somebody was going to solve it. In retrospect that was probably the most important thing we did.

Q: Was there some moment in time that was the most difficult for you?

A: There were so many of them, it would be hard to identify an individual one. I mean, it was the classic case of not knowing what you're getting into or you wouldn't have done it. ·

Again, the problem with the original idea of FedEx is that it was a network. And a network has to have a minimal level of traffic in order to break even and make money. So you go through a significant bucket, but then once you get over the top, it's quite gratifying because each incremental unit of revenue goes to the bottom line at a very fast rate. And that's what happened to FedEx.

Q: It must have been harrowing in those early months. How did you deal with the emotional upheaval?

A: Well, you've got to remember that everybody is a product of their past. I had been in the Marine Corps and in Vietnam, and so what we were really talking about here was money. We weren't talking about life and death issues. So I think that I was able to keep that in perspective. I think had I not had that perspective, I'm sure I would have been much more emotionally flattened by the difficulties of putting the company together. But once having started it and gone down the road, you know, like most entrepreneurs you're a little bit crazy and you're driven towards the end goal. Thankfully, that provides a lot of adrenaline.

Q: Crazy like a fox?

A: Well, I don't know. I would have done things a lot smarter if I'd been crazy like a fox.

Q: Like what?

A: Well, I just think that I could have made some additional decisions that would have made it less traumatic, but there's no second-guessing.

Q: Decisions about capital, ideas, or what?

A: Well, I might have made some different decisions on going slightly slower or might have made some compromises on some of the equipment that we used. I mean, just tactical decisions. At the end of the day I think most of the big decisions were right.

Q: Let's talk about risk for a moment. Risk is what makes an entrepreneur different, what sets him apart from someone else. The ability to take risk. But, of course, there are two kinds of risk. There are foolish risks and there are wise ones. Talk a little bit about your view of risk and what kind of risk it takes to be a successful entrepreneur.

A: In my mind, the biggest risk that an entrepreneur has to face is *internal*. They have to decide that this is the thing that they want to do with their time and their life more than any other thing. Because most new ideas meet a significant amount of resistance. It may be the resistance of the marketplace. It may be the resistance of the capital markets. It may be the resistance of a strong, well-entrenched competitor, but it takes almost a zealotry to get most important ideas from the incubation stage to a level of sustainable success. There are a lot of them that have initial success and then can't sustain it.

So, I think that somebody that wants to be an entrepreneur has to cross that bridge first and foremost. And that is much more important than a lot of the mechanistic things that the entrepreneur has to do. They have to really soul search and say, 'Am I totally committed to working these seven-day-a-week,

month-after-month work sessions to get this idea to success?'
And that's not for everybody.

Q: Once you get past the commitment that's required, you
have the problem of raising capital. If someone has a wonderful
idea without capital are they finished?

A: It depends on the idea. I mean, I've always envied those
people that have ideas that require no capital assets that are just
intellectual property—software, for instance. I think it's relatively easy to raise capital for that kind of venture. Hopefully, to
some degree, FedEx's success and other start-ups have shown
people that a lot of times you can make a huge amount of
money funding start-up organizations.

There is a big industry today that provides venture capital to
entrepreneurs. And I don't think that that's much of a barrier
anymore. It was when we started. But not today. So, I think if
you have a good idea and a good story and good management
you can get capital.

Q: Was there ever any point in time when you wanted to
throw in the towel or you even considered throwing in the
towel?

A: Well, there were certainly a lot of traumatic moments. But,
again, in perspective against what I'd done in the service and in
Southeast Asia, the traumas seem relatively manageable. So I

don't recall any time that I just wanted to chuck it all. But I'm sure there must have been several.

Q: Along the way, were there inspirations to you, people from other businesses that inspired you or acted as a sort of role model?

A: I don't know that I had a role model, I just had this vision of what I wanted to do. I mean, I felt that what we were trying to do would revolutionize the way business operated. And that it was a very important societal development. And I think probably putting it on that higher plane—I mean, I didn't do it just to make money. It was, 'This needs to be done. This has got to be the way that the world operates.' And, of course, it is the way the world operates today.

FedEx is to the computer age what the clipper ships were to the nineteenth century. I mean, we're the railroads and the barge lines for the ship manufacturers and the fashion goods industries. Any high value-added, high-tech industry today relies on FedEx or the express networks that have been developed to compete with FedEx to sell and source every place today.

So, I think that original thought was such a powerful driving force for me that it made a lot of the pain bounce off, I guess.

Q: Now, you mention the clipper ship, which did disappear after a while.

A: Well, the clipper ship disappeared, but perhaps that's a poor analogy. The clipper ship was just the development in its day of the fastest mode of transport for a particular market.

I don't think we are modally or technology-dependent. In other words, if somebody comes along with a machine that allows us—like Scotty did—to beam things up, we'll have one of them. We won't just stick with clipper ships and be superseded by the new technology.

Q: How do you follow the success of your initial idea with new ones? Across industries, the pace of change is so much dramatically faster than it was, say, even 25 years ago. What is next, and how do you keep your eye, not only on your own business, but on what's coming down the pike?

A: Well, I think the biggest challenges that we've had in recent years that are a natural progression from the early concepts of FedEx have been globalization and the information revolution. Just as we were designed to serve the information revolution, we have become its child, as well. We are first and foremost today a massive, on-line information network which has a lot of physical assets attached to it and a lot of wonderful people. And without that very, very advanced information-processing infrastructure, we could not do on the scale what we are currently doing.

And then the second challenge—which has been very difficult to recognize that the sectors which we serve are the primary movers of the global economy. The high value-added and high-technology industries are growing everywhere much, much faster than the rate of growth of traditional industry. Semiconductors are growing much faster than the manufacture of asphalt or lumber. So, we had to become global in nature. And that meant another enormous fight against the established order of things, because the system we wanted to put in place around the world didn't fit the traditional regulatory regime. And that's taken a lot of effort.

Over the last ten years those have been the two driving forces—the globalization and the information intensity that allowed us to rise to the next level.

Q: You've been an astute user of new information technology as it comes along. How do you evaluate it when you see it? How do you analyze which technologies will work best for you?

A: Well, first and foremost I think I should say in the interests of full disclosure I'm not a technologist and I certainly am not an expert in information and telecommunications technology. I'm literate in it. I understand, I think, what the state-of-the-art is, what it can do for you, and where it's going. And within that context, I think I have had the benefit of working with some of the smartest people in the information and telecommunications technologies in the country and in the world. One of our chief information officers is now the CIO of AT&T. One of our former business partners ran McCaw Cellular and now is the CEO of Netscape.

So, those are people that are very well known to the modern information community. So, it's been an understanding of what we needed to do with the information technology and basically what it could do. And then getting very, very good people who were comfortable with operating in that state-of-the-art or pioneering area that's allowed us to keep ahead in terms of information expertise.

Q: As for the pace of change, business cycles seem to be compressed nowadays. Everything happens so much faster, more quickly. What are the consequences of this? Do you think that the race is always to the swift? Do you think there's an overload point at which you can't do anything any faster than it's already being done?

A: I think at the end of the day, the concept that time is money is true. If you go back and you look at the pace of business today, it has a direct, lineal relationship to some work that was done by Professor Forrester at MIT, I think now almost 40 years ago.

In essence, what he showed is that a lot of business activity doesn't add any value. It's simply intermediate stages in the production or distribution of a product or a service which doesn't do anything for the customer. And, of course, the Japanese picked that up in the famous 'Can dan,' or 'just in time' management techniques. The quality movement was also a big part of speeding things up because by making things faster it exposed defects. The fact is, the faster the operation can take place—the faster the cycle—the better it's going to be from a competitive and from a quality point of view.

Now there are some businesses that probably try to go faster than the value added justified. I mean, I don't think in certain grocery products that you can add a lot of value by speeding up the process. But in most businesses you can. But I think that more and more of the business activity is in the latter category rather than in the former category. Because it's the growth sector of the economies around the world.

Q: So it's not going to slow down any? We're going to keep speeding up and keep moving faster?

A: Well, I mean, just think about some of the more prosaic things that we're going to do. I mean, let's say we go buy a pair of jeans. If you can make the purchase of those jeans faster with a higher quality component, you can win and your competitors lose. If you go into the shop to buy a pair of jeans, if they don't have a broad enough selection that allows you to get the fit and the finish or whatever that you want, then the shop has lost a sale and you'll go elsewhere to buy a competitor's product.

But if through the use of fast logistics you can have a bigger inventory in stock, a bigger variety at less investment, and then feed that inventory back in there, you'll get profitability in a number of different ways. Number one, you get more sales. Number two, you have less invested working capital in inventory. And three, you have a happier customer and bigger market share.

So most businesses, if they can be speeded up, beat companies that don't do those things.

Q: One of the trickiest things for an entrepreneur to do is to take his experience as an entrepreneur and apply it to management. Two different skill sets are very difficult for some people to make the transition. What do you think the trick or the key is to making that transition work?

A: Discipline. I think you have to understand what makes a good entrepreneur and what makes a good manager and have the discipline to follow those principles.

Q: So, let's start with the entrepreneur. What makes a good entrepreneur?

A: Well, I think an entrepreneur has to have the ability to see things that other people don't—that can view what might be rather than what is. That generally is what leads to the entrepreneurial opportunity to begin with—to look at something in a different way than people have traditionally looked at it.

And then I think secondarily what's required is enormous conviction and commitment to take the concept or idea and bring it to fulfillment. On the managerial side of the house I think there's a whole body of literature that shows people how to be effective managers. That's a learned skill. And so the primary requirement is to understand what those skills are and then have the discipline to apply them.

Q: List a couple of the skills that you think are important to good management.

A: Well, one of the most important things about any managerial position is organization. I mean, you have to be organized. You have to develop a business plan. You have to develop a staffing plan. You have to develop a marketing plan. I mean, it goes back to Henri Fayol, the French student of management that developed the thing that we all learned in school—plan, organize, staff, direct, and control. I mean, that's as true today in the high-tech sector as it was in making steel. Now, there are a lot of people who would like to wish that weren't the case, that we could sort of be free form and existential on a daily basis. It sounds much more fun, but the principles of organization and management are very well known. They've been applied for a long time, at least over the past 75 or 80 years, probably originally developed in the industrial sector for the railroads and then refined by many, many organizations, sometimes successfully, sometimes gravitating into bureaucratic gridlock which kills the organization.

But there is a strong body of academic understanding about what makes effective managers, and it just simply takes the willingness to learn those and the disciplines to follow it.

Q: So you think discipline is key?

A: Absolutely. I mean, for instance, the bigger the organization gets, the more important it is to staff effectively and to delegate. And if you are the type of person that does not have the self-discipline to delegate to someone a lot of authority—and that means, by the way, to be willing to countenance their making a mistake or two—you cannot be effective as a manager above a certain level.

So I don't think that the kinetic traits of an entrepreneur preclude that person being an effective manager, and I certainly don't think that someone who's an effective manager is precluded from being an entrepreneur. Certainly not within the corporate structure. And more recently, I think there's a lot of recognition that downsizing and delayering and one sort of corporate reengineering or another is important. But at the end of the day, it's entrepreneurship with development of new products and services, even inside large organizations, that determines who wins and who loses.

Q: And that means innovation?

A: Absolutely.

Q: Now, is thinking of innovations within an organization structure different from thinking of the first big idea or is it the same thought process that goes on, the same vision?

A: I think it's the same thought process—to look at business problems. Looking at issues in a different perspective and from a different viewpoint. What can we do differently to innovate to make this better, less expensive, more utilitarian? And I think that happens every day.

Q: Do you think it's harder to be an innovative thinker once you're entrenched in the corporate environment than it would be to be an entrepreneur and just be thinking on some sort of grand scheme?

A: It's certainly harder because the maintenance of the organization requires a great deal of energy of and by itself. A lot of people think, 'Well, I can be sort of looking ahead and have somebody else worrying about those day-to-day things and won't be encumbered by that.' It doesn't really work that cleanly. And there's a lot of baggage that you drag along with you from the past or from today's operations that has to be considered when you want to innovate into the future, particularly in large organizations. You may have made the decision years ago to put in one type of system and now, to innovate, you need a different type of an information architecture.

Well, you can't just pretend that the system that you have in place doesn't exist. So, you have to accommodate past decisions when you set out to innovate.

Q: You mention your baggage that you carry along. You had two tours of duty in Vietnam. It was obviously a formative experience. What was that like and how does it continue to contribute to your makeup today?

A: Well, I think that one of the things that I learned in my experience in the service is how people *think* that drive our trucks, that load our planes, that aren't necessarily in the managerial or the entrepreneurial world. I mean, there are people that are necessary to make a product or service that often don't have the same background or the same aspirations and views of the people that run the organization. And there very often is a very big disconnect between those people.

Now, in the last several decades I think you've seen much more emphasis in the corporate world on leadership. I would define leadership as the art of getting a group of individuals to put their individual efforts towards organizational goals. And I think the sociologists or the psychologists would call that an expenditure of discretionary effort—the minimum level of discretionary effort is what you have to do today to keep from getting fired. And the maximum discretionary effort you could put into the enterprise is the very best job that you could do today.

So, people have found out that if you have good leadership in a corporate setting, it can be worth a lot of money. And people are taking it a lot more seriously today. The athletic and the military worlds have known this for years—for centuries in the case of the military, because at the end of the day what is a military effort than the sublimation of individual goals and objectives like, 'I'd like to stay alive today,' organizational goals? And I think that understanding a lot about leadership and management of, say, a blue-collar work force to use the term that's generally used, has proven invaluable to me in what I do.

Now, that might not be necessary if I were in banking or software. But this is a transportation business that's combined with a lot of high-tech and very sophisticated assets to produce the value chain for our customers. So you have to have a clear understanding of what your work force is trying to achieve.

Q: What would you say is the hardest thing that you've ever had to do in your career?

A: Well, a number of the decisions are those where you have to make sort of right turns or you have to go a different direction and the road map's not very clear. You can't get it out of a spreadsheet. You can't get it out of a business book. You can't get it out of an advisor or your board. It's just that you've reached the point where now you've got to go off on a different path. We've had that happen several times inside FedEx.

A good example of that might be the recognition back in the late 1970s that we simply could not perform at the level of our customers' expectations unless we developed this massive information and technology system. Well, as a liberal arts major that was a fairly daunting challenge to me. So, the question was how to go about achieving that. You get the very best folks that you can to do it. And then you've got to be willing to take some risks, and go out there and get on the frontier. And, of course, we did and now almost everybody in the world has seen these little handheld computers that our couriers have and the little data-links in the trucks and how we keep up with millions and millions of things every day on a real-time basis. That all evolved from that essential understanding that we had to become a huge information and telecommunications network, as well as a huge transportation system.

So, those kinds of leaps, if you will, are the toughest business decisions you have to make because there is no road map.

Q: Looking back when you started the company in 1973, did you think then that you would be where we are now?

A: I don't know. I thought that what we were trying to do was very important and it was going to change the way people operated certain businesses. But I doubt that I thought that it was going to be a hundred and twenty some thousand people or the size and scope it is today.

Q: So you thought you would probably have a lot more competitors than you do now?

A: You know, I think that the thought of the competitors at the time didn't occupy as high a position in my mind as perhaps it should have in retrospect because the concept was so different from what anybody had done. I really didn't see where the competition was going to come from. And the way the competitor universe developed was traditional transport companies, that didn't do things the way we did at all, simply adapted their systems to be more similar to ours. And a lot of them fell along the wayside, so today it's really a small group of competitors that provides the type of services which we provide.

Q: Would you rather go up against an able competitor or one that is, you know, shall we say less than able? Which do you think is the bigger challenge?

A: Well, the most frustrating thing, of course, is to go up against a nonsensical competitor—a competitor that really is being driven not by economic decisions but by personal or survival-type stimuli. That's the toughest. So I guess I would prefer to go up against an able competitor because they make logical decisions.

Q: You can count on those?

A: Right. Right.

Q: Would you do it again?

A: Well, at my age now, maybe not. But I probably would—probably would one way or another. Just, hopefully, do it smarter.

Q: What would your advice be to someone who was looking to bring the kind of massive change to American business that you did? What would your advice be to the entrepreneur who's looking at that big idea right now about executing it?

A: I think I'd probably say that you have to evaluate very carefully whether you've got the personal commitment to do it. All we have as human beings at the end of the day is time. I mean the material things we have are pretty small compared to the value we put on our time. If you don't believe that, just ask somebody that's ill at the end of their life what they would pay for another year or two and it's probably pretty much everything they have. And when you're young you don't have those time boundaries, but as you get older they become more important.

So I think first and foremost, somebody's got to decide that this is something they're willing to be committed to and they're not going to do some of the things that perhaps they would enjoy doing from a strictly personal point of view. That they've got to derive a lot of their satisfaction and their fun from the entrepreneurial activity. If they can't cross that bridge, then they shouldn't go over to the other side. Because it is almost always an all-consuming effort.

I mean, you have people like Bill Gates—my goodness, he's incredibly successful—the most successful man probably in the late twentieth century in terms of business, but from what I understand he puts in lots of long days and lots of hours and enjoys it. So, it's that commitment and it's certainly not the money at that stage I wouldn't imagine.

Q: So it's not the money? It's for the personal satisfaction?

A: Rarely have I seen an entrepreneur achieve a major accomplishment having money be the primary driver. These people are usually driven by a vision—by a desire to change the way the world works, because they enjoy what they're doing. That sort of thing. I think that's the primary entrepreneurial factor.

Q: In the Pantheon of entrepreneurs—who would you put as those that you admire the most?

A: Oh, there's a long line of them. One of them that's one of my favorites is right here in our headquarters city of Memphis—Mr. Abe Plough of Schering-Plough who developed Coppertone and St. Joseph aspirin. He lived well into his 90s and used to call me by to see him every three or four months and generally repeat the same things to me, but he was a very, very wise man and had a lot of good advice. I enjoyed him.

Q: What was some of the advice he gave you?

A: Well, he used to say to me all the time, 'Son, you know what the secret of being in a good business is?' And I'd say, 'No, Mr. Plough.' And he'd say, 'Be in a good business.' So, you've got to be in a good business. I mean, there are a lot of terrible businesses, and, you know, don't expect to make it a great business unless it's a good business. He used to say, 'Now remember, your assets go up and down and your liabilities always stay the same. They don't go up and down.' Things of that nature. He just was a very straightforward man who had thought a lot about the fundamental principles of business.

Well, there are lots of others, you know, that I admire from an academic standpoint. Certainly you have to admire Bill Gates and Tom Watson in his day and Robert Woodruff down at Coca-Cola. I also admire greatly Collet Woolman who built Delta Airlines because he was a very self-effacing man and was keenly aware of the dangers that a founder can have on an organization if he doesn't develop good solid management to carry on after him. There have been a lot of founders who have left a legacy of very weak management that gets the organization into trouble later.

Q: What keeps you awake at night worrying? Is there anything on the horizon that you see as the biggest worry to you?

A: Well, I don't stay up at night, you know, thinking about business problems. I mean, I enjoy what I'm doing and I think I put it in an appropriate perspective but my biggest concern I think in the foreseeable future is that, as a global society, we have to come to a common set of agreements on the way the world's going to operate. And we're not really there today. I think there are a lot of risks in a lot of parts of the world— China, as it's emerging and so forth with very different views of the way economic activity should be conducted. And I don't think that the global economy can meet what most people want it to do unless there is that agreement.

I mean, just imagine what the United States would have been if, in the early days of the country, they hadn't established the fact that New York couldn't have tariffs on the people from Pennsylvania who wanted to sell things in Massachusetts. The same thing's really going on today, with the trade frictions in China and Japan. Those have to be solved by a general consensus among the governments of the world or there will be a lot of problems that evolve from it.

Q: But executives like you who do business in these countries can certainly contribute to it.

A: Well, I think that it's essential that the people running businesses that are global in nature have to work very hard for the common interest to understand the benefits of making the pie bigger rather than trying to slice up an existing pie into bigger pieces for me. And that's hard to do because it means that a lot of entrepreneurial chaos results. I mean there are winners and losers in any type of entrepreneurial market-based environment. And there are a lot of places around the world where people aren't willing to let that happen still, even though it's clear that that's the best way to advance human activity.

Q: Even though you say you're not a technology person, it is remarkable that you founded this company based on what you saw as the technology age, when the computer was coming into the forefront. What do you see as the next big thing?

A: Well, I think people have not recognized yet what a powerful engine of change the Internet will be. I think it is going to allow people to sell and source things without regard to time and place. That's never been true in the history of the world. It's going to put tremendous pressures on middlemen everywhere. It's going to be very difficult to command a price premium when you can comparison shop anything with all of the providers anywhere.

And I think that's going to be a very big challenge for a lot of businesses. I think there's a lot of technology that's just on the horizon that's going to have profound effects on people's lives and the way society is organized. When computers can recognize your speech with a great degree of accuracy, it's going to change a lot of jobs. When handwriting can be recognized electronically with great reliability, it's going to change a lot of jobs. I think that the biotechnical revolution is going to create maybe some of the biggest challenges that humankind has ever faced.

So, the Internet is going to make time and place irrelevant and within that now-connected world economy are going to be these incredible technological developments that are going to cause a lot of societal upheaval. That's what I think is ahead of us.

Q: Do you think it'll be a fruitful time for entrepreneurs— more fruitful than the past?

A: Oh, I think it'll probably be the greatest time ever for entrepreneurs, provided the governments around the world let entrepreneurs follow their natural bent. That's really the trick, I think, for a prosperous twenty-first century. From Schumpeter to Drucker to Theodore Levitt, I mean, these observers of business over the past 50 or 60 years always identify entrepreneurial drive as the indefinable element that creates wealth. It creates value. But to be entrepreneurial you have to have the freedom to pursue those visions. And if you can't do that inside a regulatory regime, then you never get the benefit of it.

Think about FedEx. I mean, absent the changes in the regulatory regime in which we operated, we could have never existed. So, it's not just the things that government lets you do or doesn't let you do, it's the entrepreneurship and the innovation that never happens when things are managed at a governmental level.

For instance, one of the biggest things about transportation deregulation wasn't just the things that happened to the transportation companies, it was the huge revolution in inventory management that came from the just-in-time revolution. So, nobody ever saw that. Nobody in the debates about deregulation of transportation ever said, 'There are going to be billions of dollars of benefit to the economy by getting rid of old-fashioned mercantilist practices.' But they occurred as a side effect of that. So it's the things that never happened and the benefits that never occur that are the price of restraints on entrepreneurship and trade and economic activity.

Q: Obviously there are a lot of elements to success as an entrepreneur. How important is luck?

A: Oh, a big part of it. I wish I could find all of those folks that just by one stroke of luck missed out. There are so many great ideas and great stories out there, but I think luck's a big part of it, unfortunately. But that's really part of life, don't you think? Nothing you can control, but that's the way life is.

Q: And timing is a part of that, too, of course.

A: Well, timing I think is a big part of it. Although, obviously, you can control your timing a bit more than your luck. I mean, if you're unfortunate enough to become ill or have an accident or, you know, lose a valued partner or something happens—that you can't foresee. But you do have some measure of control over your timing of things.

Q: I think you've said elsewhere that if you had started Federal Express five years earlier it wouldn't have worked, and five years later it would have been so obvious that there would have been tremendous competition.

A: I think that's right.

Q: So, how do you get to have perfect timing?

A: Well, I think a lot of it is just seizing an opportunity. I mean, why was Bill Gates' timing great on developing DOS for the computer? At the time IBM decided to go into the business and they wanted to subcontract the operating system and there he was to provide it, but clearly he saw the opportunity and was willing to seize it. So, I think it's just the entrepreneurial vision has to coincide with the timing—the business opportunity. And there are a lot of examples where entrepreneurial visions had to be perpetuated over long periods of time.

Q: What do you do better or differently from your CEO counterparts?

A: Phew. Well, I have more of a sense of humor than a lot of them, I'll tell you that much. A lot of the folks that run big companies are pretty dour. Some of them aren't, but I think that's one of the things. Just sort of to keep things in perspective with just a little bit of humor about the world has stood me in good stead.

Q: Anything else?

A: I think that my abilities pale by comparison to most of the people that run big organizations, but I do think that I understand our business and I understand our customers. So, if I bring some value to the team here, I hope that's what it is.

Q: Did you ever think that FedEx would be the household name that it is—that it is now a word for getting something there overnight?

A: I didn't envision that at all, but it certainly has become that. And, of course, recently we redid the entire corporate image around that theme. I mean, to FedEx something has become a verb, and it's become a verb in Chinese as well as English. So, as Pogo once said, 'To become a great leader, find a parade and run in front of it.' So, we're simply doing what our customers want us to do. And we're FedEx.

CHAPTER THREE

PETER LYNCH

FORMER MANAGER
OF FIDELITY
MAGELLAN FUND

› › ›

PETER LYNCH

FORMER MANAGER
OF FIDELITY
MAGELLAN FUND

Peter Lynch is obsessed with the stock market. Even now, in retirement from day-to-day stockpicking, Lynch eats, breathes, and sleeps the stock market. His is an obsession that began when he was a teenager, caddying for men in the investment business who talked shop on the fairways.

Stocks have been good to Lynch over the years. A brilliant pick paid for a good bit of his college education and his entire MBA. And his stockpicking prowess has made him a famous man, instantly recognized wherever he goes. He is also an accomplished author. He has written three books with coauthor John Rothchild: *One Up on Wall Street, Beating the Street,* and *Learn to Earn,* are all about investing.

Peter Lynch was born in Boston, in 1944, the son of a school teacher. His father died when he was 10 years old; his mother had to go to work to support the family. "She was able to find a good job," he recalls. "She was lucky."

Peter got a job as well, caddying at a local golf course. It was there that he learned about the stock market and began to watch share prices move. The year was 1955.

Following his B.A. on scholarship from Boston College, and a Masters of Business Administration from Wharton, Lynch went to work at Fidelity Management & Research, the giant mutual fund company. There he began a 21-year odyssey that took him to the helm of Fidelity's Magellan Fund. Hard work, luck, and perspicacity helped him outperform the market averages for the 13 years he ran Magellan. He turned it into the nation's largest mutual fund.

Then in 1990 he retired. Why? "I left for the office at 6 A.M., six days a week for over 10 years, traveled 13 days a month. It was just too much," he recalled in an interview. Now Lynch works tirelessly for the United Way and the Catholic Charities, raising money to provide scholarships for inner-city children in Boston.

Interest in investing has exploded since Lynch first joined Fidelity. And Lynch knows all too well that investors can easily make mistakes in their investments. Such boo-boos aren't limited to the amateurs—even professionals can get sucked into them.

Lynch concedes that one of the most difficult aspects of investing is being a believer when everything around you looks ominous and gloomy. It goes smack against human nature, but periods of peril and doom are often the best times to plunge into the stock market. Indeed, Lynch reveals that he almost turned in his quote machine following the 1987 Crash. Almost. Then, three years later, gloom was back in fashion.

"I mean, 1990 was very scary," he recalls. "We had a recession, we had 500,000 troops in Saudi Arabia. We were about to fight Iraq, the third-largest army in the world. The banking system was in trouble. That scared a lot of people. But you either believe in the system and hang in there or you don't. If you don't, you shouldn't own stocks, you shouldn't own funds." An investor who got into the market in 1990 had more than doubled his money by 1996.

Peter Lynch would be the first to admit that the stock market is a humbling place. But this is one investor who's proven to be every bit the market's match.

> > >

Q: Peter, you're one of the world's most famous stock pickers. You managed the Magellan Fund for Fidelity for 13 years. During that time you beat the market average by about five times. Then you famously decided to retire at the height of your success in 1990. What have you been doing since then? How have you put your energy to work in other ways?

A: I've continued to work part-time at Fidelity where I'm vice chairman. I work a couple of days a week with the younger analysts; I'm also on the Board of Trustees. But, most of my time has been spent working with nonprofit groups helping inner-city schools, trying to help the United Way. Basically social service, community service work, some big organizations, some small. So, I've had my beggar suit on, asking for money for the past seven years rather than investing. There's a lot of problems in Greater Boston and this country.

When I retired from running Magellan, our youngest daughter was still only six, so it wasn't like my wife Carol and I could take off and go to Australia or something. So, primarily, I've tried to help out a little bit.

Q: You've also been able to leverage yourself by writing books, three so far. One of the messages in your books is that the individual investor has the ability to be as good as a professional investor in stock picking. Could you explain this concept?

A: It's a little complicated. I'm saying that in some specific cases individuals may have an edge. There are over 10,000 public companies, and people can't have an edge in all of them. But remember, all you need is a few good stocks in your lifetime. So, I'm saying the average person ought to be able to follow five or six companies, know them well. And if two or three of them are attractive, they'll do fine. I'm not saying that people wake up in the morning and say now is the time to buy IBM, now is the time to buy Eastman Kodak or some biotechnology company. But, in a few cases people can have a real edge, and that's where I'm saying they should invest.

Q: When you say a person can get to know five or six companies, how do they go about doing that? What are some of the steps they could take?

A: Well, individuals have some natural advantages. For instance, if they work in a specific industry, say the auto industry, then they have an intimate understanding of how that industry works and how the companies within that industry are faring. For instance, if you were an auto dealer around the time when Chrysler started to turn around, when the minivan was introduced, you would have seen Chrysler stock go up an enormous amount. I think it advanced 10- or 12-fold on the minivan alone. And, Ford went up dramatically when Taurus was introduced. You could have been a Ford dealer, you could have been a Buick dealer, you could have been a Honda dealer; and you saw people lined up buying the Taurus.

So, when your industry goes from terrible to mediocre to good, you might see that information three, six months ahead of the so-called professional analysts. And when it goes the other way you can walk away too. So, you've got an edge, a fundamental edge.

If you'd been in the retailing industry you would have seen Limited, you would have seen Toys 'R' Us, you would have seen Home Depot, you would have seen Wal-Mart. All ahead of the pros. I mean, these are companies that did very well and you would have seen it. And you would have seen companies that came in and folded and lost their edge. You would have seen Gap turn around twice. Pier One Imports has turned around. If you were in that industry you would have seen these turnarounds first.

Q: So, recognizing the trends within your own industry, that would be your first step. Then, would you go about researching the various companies?

A: Right. A lot of people buy stocks and they don't understand what the company does. That's a classic mistake. You ought to be able to explain to a ten-year-old in three minutes or less why you own the thing. 'The sucker is going up' is not a good enough reason. I mean, that is a reason a lot of people use. But it doesn't work. I've tried that one. You have to understand the company.

Because when the stock goes down, if you don't understand what the company does, you won't know whether to add to your holding, flip a coin, or take a walk around the block. You have to have some reason for buying, to keep monitoring it. So, understand what the company's business is, how it is doing, who their competitors are.

And then you have to look at the financial position. Some companies might be losing money, but if they have $300 million in cash and no debt, or $100 million in cash and no debt, they'll be around for awhile. So you might look at ten companies that are in trouble, but the company with the good financial condition, you could find very easily. You look at the asset side of the balance sheet, it shows lots of cash, the liabilities side shows no debt. You might be losing money but it's very hard to go bankrupt if you have no debt. So, you decide this company is going to be okay for two or three years.

Then some companies have loads of debt, no cash, they're about to blow taps on this company, it's all over. I mean, why would you want to invest in that? So, a little financial check is important.

Q: And you can find this information in the annual report?

A: Annual report or quarterly report. The quarterly report is even more current. You can get that very rapidly from companies.

Q: And once you find that the company is doing well financially, it's on solid footing, what next?

A: Well, I think you still have to say 'Why have I bought this? What is my story? What is the reason?' There might be two or three reasons. Maybe the industry has been depressed and three or four competitors are leaving the business, or the industry is consolidating. Whatever the story, it's usually unique and it's different in each case. It's different for a retailer than it is for a company that makes cement or a company that sells insurance. But, you have to have some reason, not just that the stock is cheap or that it's going to go up. There has to be something compelling.

The key element here is that when you own a stock, you own a piece of the company. The company does well, the stock does well. Take McDonald's as an example. Its earnings went up 50-fold the last 30 years. The stock has gone up over 50-fold. Coca-Cola's earnings have gone up over 25-fold. Guess what? Coca-Cola stock has gone up over 25-fold. Bethlehem Steel is earning less than they did 30 years ago. Their profits are lower than they were 30 years ago. The stock, magically, is lower than it was 30 years ago.

That's what happens. It's what's going on at the company. If the company does poorly, the stock does poorly. It's as simple as that.

Q: You mentioned that you need only a few very good companies to do well in the stock market. When you say that, what do you mean? What kind of appreciation are you looking for?

A: Well, the nice thing about stocks is that if you invest $1,000, you can make a lot more than $1,000. But all you can lose is that $1,000. I've proven that a few times. But, if you're right six times out of ten, or even five times out of ten, you can do very well. If you have six or seven companies you're following, and all of a sudden you see this one company is doing very well, they're getting better and better and better, so you keep adding to that one, and it pays off. Sometimes you can have a stock go up fivefold, tenfold, twentyfold. You need only a few really big stocks in a lifetime to make up for a lot of little mistakes.

I have great luck with stocks like the grocery store company Stop 'n' Shop, because I can understand their business. I've had a lot of luck with Dunkin' Donuts. Those are the kinds of companies I bought and five, six, seven, eight years later I said wow, look at how much they went up. These are not stocks that went up immediately. My great stocks have been great in the third, fourth, fifth year I owned them. Not my third, fourth, or fifth day, not my third, fourth, or fifth month. For some reason you lose money more rapidly than you make it. Normally your great stocks hit in the second, third, fourth, fifth year.

Q: And you should add to the position as they go up?

A: Well, at least you hold on. You don't say, 'Gee, it went up, let's get out, I'm going to buy something else.' People also think they have to buy when a company first comes public. Not true. You could have bought Toys 'R' Us three years after it was public and you could have made 15 times your money. You could have bought Wal-Mart ten years after it went public and made 30 times your money. You may have said, 'Gee, I'm very cautious, I'm going to look at this company, I want to make sure they'll go into other markets, succeed in other markets.' So you waited ten years after going public before buying it. You would have made 30 times your money. Ten years after they went public, they were in only 15% of the United States, only in small towns. They hadn't saturated the rest of the country.

So you say to yourself, wait a second, why can't they go to 17%, why can't they go to 21% of the country? Guess what? Maybe they can go to 27%. That's all they did for the next 30 years. Then they're all over the country—and that's an entirely different story. Once Wal-Marts are everywhere, they've run out of places to go, and it's a different kind of analysis. But, the company is doing very well in only a small part of the country, so it might take them three decades to spread across the country.

Q: Speaking of individual stock picks, what was your biggest winner? And how did you find it?

A: Well, I've had a couple of great stocks in my life. I certainly can remember Chrysler. Chrysler was one that was the biggest position in the Magellan Fund which I bought in 1982 after they had the guaranteed government loans. They already had a billion dollars in cash. They were about to break even at the bottom of our worst recession since World War II. They had a lot of new cars coming along. And cars in use were getting very old. You can measure these things. The average car on the highway was the oldest it had been in 15 years, according to inspections in 49 out of 50 states. So, you have to replace these old things. So, you knew at some point in time it was going to get better.

When it got better I was really surprised. The surprise to me was the minivan. That was an enormous success that came out of nowhere. They sold over 500,000 of those this year, at $6,000 of profit per van. I mean that's $3 billion on one product.

And then they compounded it when they bought American Motors and got the Jeep. And they'll sell a couple hundred thousand of those at a $5,000 profit each; that's another billion. And those were surprises. They're the part of the story that kept you saying wow, new things are happening here, so it got better and better.

Another great stock was Hanes. It was a great story. My wife came home with this one. They test-marketed L'Eggs pantyhose in Columbus, Ohio, and in Boston and a few other markets, I think. And my wife brought this product home and said she liked it. I did a little bit of research, not a lot. I find the average woman goes to the supermarket or a drugstore once or twice a week. They go to a department store once every five weeks.

And all the hosiery being sold in the supermarkets and drugstores was junk, no good. These people came up with a product called L'Eggs, they sold them in drugstores. They racked them and supplied them every day, making sure all the colors were there. And it was a huge success.

This was a little company called Hanes. The stock was a very big hit for Magellan, it was a big hit for Fidelity. I think it went up tenfold. And then it was bought out by a company called Sara Lee. If they hadn't been bought out, it might have gone up 200-fold. I wish they were never bought out, but that's the way life goes.

At some point in time I thought somebody might copy what Hanes was doing. Normally when somebody is doing very well they attract copycats. I think within a year after L'Eggs was on the market, a large hosiery company called Kaiser-Roth came in with a product called No Nonsense, and put it right next to the L'Eggs rack.

I went to the supermarket and bought 50 different pairs, different sizes and different colors. They must have wondered what kind of family does this person have at home when I bought all these pairs of No Nonsense hose. My wife gave them out to friends, and I gave them out to everybody in the office, I said take them home, try them out and tell me what you think. A few of them came back in a week and said, 'It's not as good.' That was it. I held onto my Hanes. And that was a very big stock. That's what research is.

I mean, those are the kinds of stories you can understand. Look for companies that make a better product.

Q: One of the things you're known for is not investing in biotech companies. Is that because biotech is just too hard to understand?

A: It depends. There are some biotechnology companies that have actually become drug-producing companies with products on the market. They're actually changing people's lives. But, in the beginning they all had $50 million in cash, and they had 50 PhDs and 51 microscopes, and there was nothing there. It was just all sizzle, no steak.

So, it was all 'maybes' and 'we'll do this,' 'we're working in this area.' But in the last five or six years, a lot of these companies have moved to actually having earnings, like Amgen, Genetics Institute, Genzyme, Biogen. These are real companies today, they're analyzable. Back in the 1980s, they were just a bunch of dots. Which one is going to win you didn't know.

I usually stay away from companies that have no sales, no earnings, and a lot of hope. That's not my field.

Q: One of the most difficult parts of investing for the average individual is seeing that the moment when you should be buying stocks—Chrysler for you in 1982—is exactly when everything looks the darkest and the gloomiest. It's the time when you say 'I'm not going near that.' How can an individual go against that psychologically powerful mindset?

A: It's not easy. In this business everybody has got the brain power to do the work, because this stuff is not hard. The key organ is the stomach. Are you ready for the declines? Because when the market declines, usually the background noise is not positive. People are being laid off, or somebody's rumored to be laying people off. Sometimes real estate prices are weak, or there are a lot of political problems. I mean, 1990 was a very scary year. We were in a recession, we had 500,000 troops in Saudi Arabia. Here we were about to fight Iraq, the third-largest army in the world, and they were supposed to be tough. And the banking system was in trouble. Commercial banks were in trouble. Now they're in great shape, but in 1990 they weren't.

There was not a lot of pleasant background noise. That scared people. You either believe in the system, you say 'America is going to be okay ten years from now, 20 years from now, 30 years from now.' If you believe in the system, you hang in there. If you don't, you shouldn't own stocks, you shouldn't own funds.

Q: So, is there a specific point at which you say 'things are looking very grim, time to buy'?

A: Well, that's not a reason to buy; that's a reason to say there's potential here. What can go right? You know, we've had nine recessions since World War II, none of them turned into Depression. There are always people saying, 'We're going to have a depression.'

We had lots of depressions before the Great Depression. We had six or seven. This was not the only one. Why have we not had another depression since then? Things like Social Security were helpful, unemployment compensation was helpful. We have bank deposits insured, we have the Federal Reserve that's on the ball. I mean, there are a lot of checks and balances.

There are only 18 million people in the manufacturing sector today. So, when the economy gets hurt it's not as big a drop as it used to be. The average recession has resulted in a 2%

decline in employment. The worst we had was a 3% decline in 1981–82. It's not the scale we used to have, but we do have recessions. They're going to happen in the future. There's no reason to expect they won't happen again. But, when they start, people think it's going to be a depression. They'll say their mother or their aunt or their uncle said, 'You know, in the Depression Uncle Joe had to sell apples,' or, 'Sister Suzy was selling pencils.' It must have been a great decade to buy apples and pencils because you always hear these stories about the Depression.

And that's in the back of your brain. You laugh about it when the stock market is going up. But, when the market starts to go down, and you hear on the radio and telephone and the press about how bad things are, you start to say 'Oh my goodness, my grandmother was right and my mother was right. I should never own stocks; I'm going to get wiped out.'

Less than 1% of Americans owned stocks in 1929. I mean, it was not that big a deal. The stock market did not cause the Depression. You just had a full-scale economic decline, and there were no buffers in the economy.

Q: Contrarily, when things are going great, does that mean that it's time to think about selling? We've had a very big bull market now for a long time. Knowing when to sell is another tough question for individual investors.

A: I think market timing is a waste of time. It's futile, it's ineffective. I mean, from 1965 to 1995, over those 30 years, if you had the amazing luck of picking the low day of the year in the stock market, let's say you put $1,000 in, you're lucky, you find the low day of the year, you put your $1,000 in.

Some poor soul found the high day of the year—managed somehow always to put $1,000 in on the high day of the year in the market. And the third individual put $1,000 in at the first day of the year. The difference between the three? Not that much. The person investing at the high of the year had a 10.6% return. The person investing at the low of the year had 11.7%. The person investing the first day of the year had 11%. It wasn't that big of a difference.

And what are the odds of picking a high day versus a low day? Very limited. The difference was just one percentage point between the high of the year and the low of the year. So, trying to time the market doesn't work. If you had only missed being in the stock market 40 months the last 40 years, your return would be around 2% rather than the 12% return if you'd been in the market for the entire 40 years.

So, trying to say what months are going up, when they're going down, jumping around, it's counterproductive. You either believe in it or you don't. The market may be wrong for some people.

Let's say somebody has saved a lot of money. They've saved $60-$70-$80,000, a huge amount of money. They're about to send their one kid or two kids off to college, and it's one year from now, or it's six months from now. If they're going to put their money into mutual funds or into stocks, with a six-month horizon, that's wrong. What if the market goes down? If it goes down a lot, you might have to put up another $60-$70-$80,000. That's not the right horizon.

I get people call me up and say, 'Joey is going to school in a year. Can you tell me a fund to buy? I don't want a lot, just gains of 35 to 40%, you know. No risk, though, it can't go down.' I say, we don't have those products, they don't exist. Your horizon is wrong. You need to look 10 years, 20 years down the road. I mean, it's a common mistake, people are saving to get a down payment on a house, and they want to slip it in the stock market for a quick six-month return. That doesn't work.

And there's a reverse to that. Some people retire at 62 or 65, and they say, well, now I've got to own nothing but money markets. Well, if you're married and you're 65, one of you is going to make it to 92, so you have a very long-term horizon. To just be in money market funds isn't right either. You should have some of your money in the stock market, if you believe that corporate profits will be higher, 10 years from now, 20 years from now, 25 years from now. Because the stock market will be higher. That's why stocks work.

Q: Let's talk a little bit about mutual funds. We've seen an incredible boom in the business. Americans are buying funds in record numbers, record dollars are going into them. You mentioned that people don't understand that there are risks associated with them. How many people, do you think, do not understand that when you buy a government securities fund, or Ginnie Mae as it's called, that they can lose money?

A: I'm afraid people don't understand with bonds either. They buy a fund that just invests in U.S. government bonds and they say, 'No credit risk, government guaranteed,' well, that's government-guaranteed principal. Now, if interest rates go up, say, long-term bonds are at 8%, and inflation picks up and rates go to 11%, that bond is going down, your fund is going down.

At maturity, you'll get your money back. But, if you have a 30-year bond, that's a long wait. And the bond market is quite volatile. Just because you own government bonds doesn't mean they can't go up or down. So, I think you should understand that—if you have a short-term bond of two or three years, it's not a problem. But, if you own 10-, 15-, 20-, 30-year bonds, U.S. government or any kind of bonds, they are volatile. And people need to realize that.

It's just like a mortgage. When rates go down, people refinance their mortgage. And when rates go up they're very happy about it. Well, if you own a bond, when rates go up you're not happy about it. You're on the other side of that equation.

Q: And, of course, none of the funds are backed by the government as a bank account is. Do you think that people have misconceptions about bank CDs and funds being backed by the government?

A: I'm not sure about that. I think people are very comfortable with money market funds. And there's little risk there. But, if they're investing in bond funds, they can have eight-, nine-, ten-year maturities, they can have 50-year maturities. And be very volatile.

Stock funds, of course, are all over the place. In the past 95 years, on 50 occasions, the market's declined 10% or more. We've had 50 declines in 95 years. So, that's about once every two years, the market has experienced a 10% decline. We call that a correction: a euphemism for losing a lot of money rapidly.

But, of those 50 declines, 15 of the 50 have been 25% or more. So, once every six years the market has had a 25% decline. Now, that will get your attention, that's a big number. I mean, it's going to happen in the future. I don't know when it's going to start—two weeks from now, two months from now, four years from now—but you're going to have a decline. You have to say to yourself, what am I going to do when the market goes down? You should look in the mirror and say what am I going to do? If you're going to cash out, you don't have the right temperament for the stock market, and you shouldn't be there. That's fine. I'm not recommending everybody be in stocks. I think they're the best place to be. But maybe you shouldn't be there.

Q: In a previous interview you said that you almost traded in your Quotron after the 1987 crash. What made you feel that way? Obviously it was a very disruptive, dismal time. Are you glad you didn't?

A: I think the issue was the market just went too far, too fast. I think people forget that in August 1982, the Dow Jones industrial average stood at 777. It took four years to get to 1700, then in 1986, it goes from 1700 to 2700 in 11 months. And then in three months it goes back to 1700. It drops 1,000 points in three months, 508 points in one day. So, it's gone sideways, at 1700 for a year. No one worried about losing 1,000 points in nine months, but 1,000 points in three months, people say, 'Oh my God, the market has crashed.' But it was exactly the same place it was a year before. If it had gone—you know, if it had gone from 777 to 1700, stayed there for one year, no one worried. It blew out an incredible burst of speed to 2700, then declined to 1700, people said this is the end of the world. Stocks went from 50 to 12, 50 to 35, people were just tossing them in. The companies were doing fine.

The 1987 Crash wasn't anywhere near as scary as 1990. You call up companies, they say we're doing fine, business is good, we have a good balance sheet, we're buying our shares. In 1990, companies were not doing well. They said our economy is slowing down, we sent 500,000 troops to Saudi Arabia, the banking system was in trouble. I mean, 1990 was a lot scarier than 1987. But, just the people looking at the stocks, looking at the market, trying to think of the market saying we're going to have a Crash. Well, they had one.

But, then they think there was going to be another drop. When it went to 1700 they thought it might go back to 700.

Q: So, you did not hand in your quote machine?

A: I pounded it a few times.

Q: The year 1990 was also the year you quit. Was this a reaction to the dreary market?

A: Not at all. I certainly didn't predict very well, because the market has more than doubled since then. I just thought, you know—I was leaving for the office at 6 A.M. six days a week, and I was traveling 12, 13 days a month. And I hadn't seen much of my wife or my three kids for eight or nine years. And I wanted to do other things too. I wanted to be involved in a lot of charities. So, I had to cut back on the job. I loved the job. It's a great company, great job. I had one out of every 100 Americans in my fund.

These were people that I'd meet in airports and they had made a total of $7,000 and they were ecstatic about it, it made a difference in their life. It was very fulfilling to meet these folks. That's why I worked so hard.

Q: Do you remember any story in particular that anyone told you?

A: I met people everywhere. I met somebody at the Grand Ole Opry. I met them in parking lots at theaters and in churches. They'd come up and say, 'Thank you very much. We paid off the mortgage,' or 'We sent somebody to college.' I get thousands of letters. Oh yeah, I remember lots of stories.

Q: What a wonderful payoff.

A: Incredible. Thank God the market went up, it was great. If it hadn't, I would have had to dye my hair and move to Fiji.

Q: Let's talk about Magellan. It was and is now the world's largest mutual fund, and it certainly was when you were running it, partly because of your stock-picking prowess.

How did it change for you going from a relatively small or medium-sized fund into the behemoth that it became? What was it like to manage?

A: Well, it didn't change a lot. You still have to buy companies and have them go up. And some of the big stocks I had were like Fannie Mae, Chrysler, Boeing, Ford Motor company. So, there are a lot of big companies out there that a big fund could buy. I mean, the New York Stock Exchange is worth over $5 trillion. If you look at the Nasdaq you're talking another couple of trillion. If you look at the big stocks overseas, we're talking another $3 trillion. These are big numbers. So, managing $15 billion or $30 billion or $50 billion is not a very big part of a $10 trillion industry.

Q: But isn't it harder to move around?

A: Oh, it's harder. You just have to be right. I mean, it's harder to put money to work when you have to buy three million shares instead of 3,000. And that's one reason that the public can invest on their own; if they want to buy, all they have to do is buy 300 shares. They don't have to buy 3 million or 4 million or 7 million.

Q: It almost sounds like you're recommending that people buy individual stocks themselves rather than mutual funds.

A: Well, I think they can do both. Some people have the personality and the skills to pick individual stocks and they're also ready to go to work. It is not a game; they have to be able to do some work. And if they can withstand the volatility in the market that we talked about, they could do well on their own.

I don't know how to use a computer, but my three daughters do, my wife Carol does. Imagine all the people who use computers, who know something about computers. Three years after Microsoft became public, you could have bought the stock and made 40 times your money.

I mean, somebody who is familiar with computers should be able to figure out that MS-DOS, Microsoft's operating system, is working. I don't know whether IBM is going to win, Dell Computer is going to win, or Compaq. But guess what, they see that Microsoft is a software, that it's the operating system everybody uses. I didn't own it, I missed it. But, lots of people should have seen it. That's their business. They saw it happening. And that's the kind of investing I'm talking about.

Q: Peter, should people own stocks, or should they own mutual funds?

A: I think they should do both. I think an average investor is going to have a few opportunities every decade to find some big stocks. That can really make a difference in your life. You know, you put a few thousand dollars in some stock, and it goes up tenfold, it gets your attention. They don't come along all the time. But, they're out there looking for you. I mean, there are great companies coming along, you'll see them if you're willing to do some homework. If you're not willing to do that exercise, to do some homework, then mutual funds might be the right thing for you. Buy an equity mutual fund. That might be something that's good for some people. You can also do both.

And maybe some people don't want to do either. That's fine too. I just want people to do it, when they do it in a civilized way. And some people are buying equity funds, and they buy the Japanese fund one month, and there's the Korean fund and they flip to the Germany fund. Then they buy a biotechnology fund. I mean, that's speculating, that's gambling. That's like going to a casino except there's more paperwork. That's not investing.

The same kind of thing people do when they buy a car or they buy a refrigerator should work in the stock market, does work in the stock market. This is not a game. Whoever invented that term 'play the market' did a lot of damage. It's not play.

Q: Could you define what a mutual fund is?

A: A mutual fund is the vehicle for small investors to combine their money into a larger pool to get professional management and diversification at low cost. It's hard to buy 20 stocks with $1,000. It's hard to buy 100 stocks. The commissions would kill you. So, with a fund you get diversification, and you can get a specific purpose. Maybe you just want to buy emerging growth companies. Maybe you want to have some of your money in emerging markets, some of these small countries around the world, that are growing very rapidly.

Or, you want to just buy something now like electronics or technology. So, that's why a mutual fund works. They can pool their money, get professional management. So, you get the advantages of being a large investor. And you can get in and out every day, if you want. You're not locked up.

Q: So, in effect, given the boom in mutual funds, the individual who is in the fund is now driving the markets in a way that never happened before. Traditionally, the institutional investor, that is, the professional, drove the market. How do you think this has changed the way the market works, if at all?

A: Well, so far we've had a couple of tests. I mean, one day in 1991, the market fell over 200 points. We had a 1990 drop that was substantial, almost 25%. We had a rough go in 1996, the market fell very sharply. It almost fell 10% one day, it was down dramatically. The public hasn't panicked. They didn't say oh my goodness, it's the end of the world and cashed everything out. I think they learned something from '87. You know, the people that sold in '87—the people in the market who borrowed money, or were in options—got in trouble. They were the people hurt in '87. The people that held on were happy a year later, two years later, three years later.

I think people have learned to stay with it. And at some point if the market goes from 6,000 to 28,000—at some place the market gets out of line. Between 1942 and 1995 the market has sold at prices between 10 and 20 times corporate earnings.

${Q}$: That means the average price of the stock is 10 to 20 times what the average company is earning?

${A}$: If the company is earning $10 a year and the stock's at $50, it's five times earnings; if they're earning $5, it's ten times earnings. If they're earning $1, it's 50 times earnings. When you do the math of the entire market, either the S&P 500 or the Dow Jones industrial average, looking at all these companies together, they sold between 10 and 20 times earnings.

When it gets outside that range you say the stock market is overpriced. When it gets under 10—it hasn't got there very often—you'd say it's an incredible giveaway. But, that's the general range. The profits of the companies in the S&P 500 have grown about 9% a year. That doesn't sound like much, but at 9% a year, money doubles every eight years, quadruples every 16 years, and goes up sixfold every 25 years. So, the profits on the S&P 500 have gone up about sixfold over the last 25 years. The stock market has gone up a little more than sixfold. There's a reason why the stock market goes up. It's called corporate profits.

As a company, when your profits go up, your stock goes up.

Now, it doesn't always go up. We've had some recessions, profits go down, interest rates go up, inflation goes up, margins get squeezed. It doesn't always happen, but my expectation is ten years from now companies will make a lot more money than they do now, 20 years from now they'll be making more money. What they do in two or three years, you don't know. That's very hard to predict. But, you're investing and you're hoping what's been true for most of the century is going to continue. That's what you're betting on.

Q: Are the American markets the best place in the world to invest?

A: There have been much better markets. I mean, the last 10, 15, 20 years—our market has done very well. I think of the leading 15 markets maybe we're number 5 or 6; we're not number 1. A lot of small markets have done much better.

The Japanese market was a lot better until the last three years. That's an example of a market that had gone up a lot, and then went to La-La land; it just went from 20,000 to 50,000, went to crazy prices relative to corporate earnings. And now it's been digesting that for three or four years, it's been tough. It should have never gone above 20,000 and it just went too high.

It's like if our market went from 6,000 to 60,000 in the Dow Jones. You'd have to say it's overpriced on what companies could earn in the next three or four years.

Q: Let's go back in time a little. In one interview you said that you spent the entire first date with your wife-to-be talking about the stock market. Were you obsessed with the stock market, or just nervous?

A: Well, maybe I had nothing else to talk about. I certainly was nervous, yeah. I guess I was talking a lot about companies that I had looked at. I had worked the summer of '66 at Fidelity and I thought it was great. Companies like Kentucky Fried Chicken were just starting out; they were exciting companies.

Intel founders, left to right: Robert Noyce,
Andrew Grove, and Gordon Moore. (Intel Corp.)

Grove shaking hands with Microsoft Chairman Bill Gates
at a meeting in Burlingame, California, November 9, 1992.
(AP/Wide World Photos, Inc., NYC)

Intel Corporation employees,
1970s. (Intel Corp.)

Close-up of a computer
chip, 1978. (Intel Corp.)

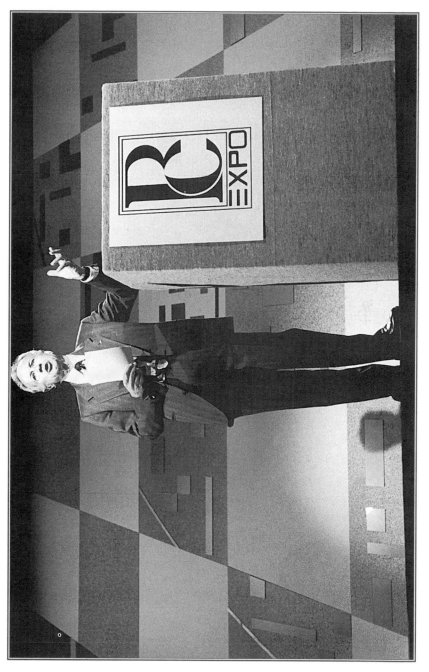

Grove delivering a keynote address during Comdex, the computer industry's biggest trade show, June 28, 1994, New York City. (AP/Wide World Photos, Inc., NYC)

Fred Smith in Little Rock, Arkansas, 1972, with his first
Federal Express Falcon jet. (*Arkansas Democrat Gazette*)

The christening of Federal Express's then-new cargo carrier, a DC10, April 1980. (*The Commercial Appeal,* Memphis, Tenn.)

Inside Federal Express's Memphis hub, 1981.
(*The Commercial Appeal,* Memphis, Tenn.)

Peter Lynch at age 16, Braeburn Country Club caddie. (Courtesy Peter Lynch)

Lynch in his Boston College graduation portrait, 1965. (Courtesy Peter Lynch)

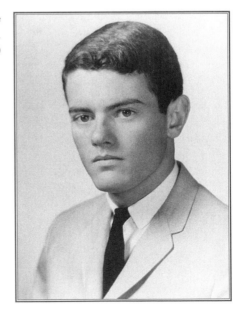

U.S. Army Lieutenant
Peter S. Lynch, 1967.
(Courtesy Peter Lynch)

Upon joining Fidelity as a
research analyst in 1969.
(Courtesy Peter Lynch)

Peter Lynch in the office, surrounded by papers and photos of his family.
(Courtesy Seth Resnick)

Peter Lynch and his wife. (Courtesy Peter Lynch)

Pleasant Rowland with children, using materials created by Rowland for The Pleasant Rowland Reading Program. (Courtesy Pleasant Rowland)

Rowland at her cottage in the north woods of Wisconsin.
(Courtesy Pleasant Rowland)

At the Madison, Wisconsin, "Concert in the Square"—
a special summer concert series started by Rowland.
(Courtesy Pleasant Rowland)

Pleasant Rowland (*top right*) before the 1995 commencement ceremony at her alma mater, Wells College. (Brantley Carroll photography)

Speaking to the Wells College class of 1995. (Brantley Carroll photography)

Rowland with American Girl Collection dolls. (Pleasant Company)

Paul Volcker as a young boy, fishing (1931). (Courtesy Paul Volcker)

Portrait as a young man. (Courtesy Paul Volcker)

The Volcker family in the 1940s, left to right, Paul Jr., Ruth, Paul, Alma, Virginia, and Louise. (Courtesy Paul Volcker)

Paul Volcker in 1958, reading to his daughter. (Courtesy Paul Volcker)

Volcker, July 1983, as Federal
Reserve Board Chairman
facing questions from the Senate
Banking Committee at the start
of his confirmation hearings for
a second term.
(AP/Wide World Photos, Inc., NYC)

With Rep. Fernand J. St. Germain, chairman of the House
Banking Committee. (AP/Wide World Photos, Inc., NYC)

That year there was an airline strike. I had to go visit companies by bus. I had to travel to Ohio and Pennsylvania by bus and back to Boston. Looking at companies and analyzing companies was exciting. I think that's what I was talking about. Not the market in general, but just how exciting companies are. There's a lot of fun involved. I mean, you look at cement companies one week, you look at aluminum companies a week later, you're looking at power companies after that. There's always some segment of the market that should be getting better or is getting better, so it's exciting.

Q: You've said you got your start in the stock market on the golf course. Explain.

A: I was very lucky. I grew up in a suburb—you know I could caddie for a job. My father took sick when I was seven, he died when I was ten. My mother had to go out to work. She was able to get a job. I mean, that was lucky. Some mothers today can't do that. She got a good job.

I started caddying at 11. When I applied for a job at Fidelity in 1965 there were, I think, 75 applicants for three spots, but I had caddied for the president for nine years. Somehow I got the job. It was the only job interview I ever took. So, that was luck. A lot of kids in the inner city don't have the opportunity I had; I was lucky.

I grew up in the 1950s. The stock market was terrific then. It was almost as good as the 1980s. It was the second-best decade of the century. And that's when I was growing up. People talked about stocks and I'd look at them three months later, six months later, a year later, and I didn't have any money to invest, but I'd noticed they'd gone up. I said gee, this is worth looking at.

Q: Do you remember one of the first stocks you owned?

A: Absolutely. I think I gathered together about $800 or $900. I had a $300 caddie scholarship to Boston College and I worked enough to pay the rest of the $1,000 tuition. I lived at home. So, I had saved up a grand total, I think, of $800 or $900 after a long time. And I bought my first stock in a company called Flying Tiger Airlines.

I did a little research on cargo trips and flying cargo. I got lucky because the reason the stock went up wasn't the business. It was that the Vietnam War started, and Flying Tigers was hauling troops and cargo. The Vietnam War made the stock go up. I think it went from 8 to 80.

Q: You made ten times your money?

A: No, I sold some at $20, I sold some at $30, but that stock basically paid for my graduate school. I think I had a Flying Tiger graduate school scholarship. But that was very exciting.

There was some other stuff I bought then that went down. I've sort of forgotten those. You know you remember your winners, they stick out a lot easier than the losers. I made a lot of mistakes too, but that one worked.

Q: Where did you go to graduate school and what degree did you get?

A: I went to the Wharton School of Finance at the University of Pennsylvania in Philadelphia. That's where I was lucky enough to meet my wife. She was an undergraduate. Very pleasant. It was a great school, and I enjoyed it.

Then I went in the army for two years after that. I was a lieutenant in the army. Went to Texas for a few months and Korea for 13. I came back to Fidelity in 1969. I was a summer employee in 1966, and came back for good in 1969.

Q: What did you start out as?

A: I was an analyst. I covered the textile industry, the metals industry, the chemical industry, car industry, a lot of basic industries. I continued to follow these industries when I became Fidelity's director of research in 1974.

Q: So you spent about five years as an analyst?

A: About five years of that, but then an additional three years of being director of research. So, I analyzed stocks from '69 to '77 when I took over the Magellan Fund.

When you're a fund manager, you're basically an analyst. You still do the same thing—looking at companies—you just look at more of them. Instead of a narrow four or five industries, you look at 200 different industries. You're always looking at companies. If you look at ten, you might find one that's interesting; look at 20, you might find two; if you look at 100, you might find 10 to investigate further.

Basically, the person who turns over the most rocks wins the game. You have to be very flexible. Some people are not flexible enough to turn over some rocks. They won't look at companies with unions, they won't look at companies whose names start with 'R,' they won't look at companies that are in dead industries. They say this industry is now broke. They only want to look at the hypergrowth industries. I look at all industries. I always think there are opportunities everywhere. To me flexibility is very important. A lot of people have prejudices and biases, they just avoid a lot of opportunities.

There was a great company called Service Corp. International. It was a funeral home company. That's all they did. It was a fantastic stock. So, this is the kind of thing some people won't look at. They just said, this is an industry going nowhere. Well, they had a great formula and they rolled with it and they did very well.

Q: What advice would you give to a person interested in getting into your business, the world of the stock market?

A: I think a young person can begin by doing a lot of this on paper, in a hypothetical portfolio. I mean, maybe you don't have any money to invest. But you could write down in three minutes or less, a couple of sentences, why am I buying this, why do I like this? Then you follow the company. And you could say gee, what I'm really good at is buying depressed companies, what I'm really good at is buying small companies. I'm really good at looking at turnarounds.

Over several years you'll find out something about yourself. You say I'm going to put $10,000 in on paper. One of the problems with some of these games they have in schools is they only last three months or six months; it's too short a period.

So, you get the annual report, you get the quarterly reports, you look at the products. A company like Nike, in 1987, you had an incredible opportunity to buy the stock. This is a company which was not doing that well in '85–'86. They started to turn around in '87. The quarterly report in the summer of '87 said orders are up dramatically, sales are getting better, earnings are up. And then the next quarterly comes out about a month before the stock market crash in October. It says orders are up dramatically, overseas looks good, balance sheet looks good, earnings are up. Then the stock market crashed and I think the stock went from 10 to like 4.

This was a great opportunity. You had the information, it was right there: Business is terrific. Three months later, they say orders are up again, very sharply, earnings are terrific. The stock was only back to $10. You could have waited three months after the break in 1987 and bought Nike and made over 12 times your money. The information was there. It was right there, saying we're doing well. And you could go to stores and see they're doing well.

Companies like Coca-Cola are in 200 countries. Johnson & Johnson is in 150 countries. So, why can't Nike sell their products all over the world? Well, guess what, they did. And that was it. They had new products and went into new markets. That was not complicated. You don't need a fancy computer to figure that out.

The information was there. You could take advantage of the decline in the market saying, 'Gee, there's a company that's getting better and it just fell in half. And here's my chance.'

So, you're like a vulture circling around waiting for these opportunities. Every now and then the market goes down, or there's a temporary problem. People dump it and you say listen, this is a temporary problem, I can explain it. They're new products, they're getting better. You wait for things to get better. You don't buy symptoms, you wait for the real thing. You say this is really improving, then you buy it. And if nothing is getting better and it's just cheap, just wait for something to happen.

You only have to own a few stocks; you don't have to own 50, you don't have to own 100. People spend so much time buying this, buying that, they chew up so much in commissions. You can lose 8%, 9% on commissions alone.

Q: The stock market can be a very humbling place. What's the biggest lesson that it's taught you?

A: Well, I think, first of all you have to know that you're going to lose money sometimes. You're going to make mistakes. I mean, when you really work hard in school, if you have all the right answers, you get a 98 on a test. Well, you know, questions like who fought in the 30 Years War, or if the boat left St. Louis going eight miles an hour and the train left Pittsburgh going ten miles an hour where would they meet. You could solve these things.

Well, the stock market isn't like that. Everything is not perfect, you have to take some risk. You have to say to yourself, by the time everything is perfect, the stock has gone from 10 to 60. Occasionally, you have to say I'm willing to take a little risk. Things are getting better, the balance sheet is okay. I'm going to buy this; I might be wrong. You can be wrong in this business maybe three or four times out of ten. But, if you're right and you hold on and you make three times your money, five times your money, ten times your money, it more than offsets the times you're wrong.

So, you have to understand you have no control when a recession is going to happen. Who knew? Our State Department didn't know Saddam Hussein was going to walk into Kuwait in 1990. They weren't ready. How are you supposed to know that? And all of a sudden, we have this terrible situation in the Gulf, we have a recession on our hands, the banking system is in trouble. How could you predict that? Obviously you couldn't.

So, you say to yourself something is going to happen. I know what's going to happen. Something in the future is going to happen that's not going to be so good. It's going to take the whole market, it's going to go down. The same thing may happen in a company—is it a real thing, is this a real change? Maybe they bought some new business or their basic business slipped, or some better competitor came along.

Then you get out, you say I was wrong. But, my methods were correct. I used the right approach. If I keep using that method, I'll prevail.

Q: You mentioned that when you sit down to write out a paper portfolio and put down stocks that you like, you learn about yourself. What have you learned about yourself in your years as a stock picker?

A: Well, I think I probably should turn in the quote machine and never have one. People spend hours, they call their broker four times a day to get quotes, and they're looking at what stocks are going up or down all day. That is an absolute waste of time.

Great companies do well, their earnings do well, and what the stock does one week or next week doesn't matter. The average stock on the New York Stock Exchange has had a 50% range between its high and its low every year. That means that a stock at $20, sold sometime in the year at $24, sold sometime in the year at $16, and finished the year at $20. But, during the year it had a 50% range. I mean, stocks move a lot. You have to get used to that and say this is the kind of volatility I'm dealing with here. That's the average stock in the New York Stock Exchange.

You can take advantage of that. Time is on your side in the stock market. If you're not on margin where you borrow the money to buy, you've got plenty of time to say 'I'm going to be right, the story is getting better. So far no one has recognized it. They will eventually.' Stocks go up when companies' earnings go up, not because of buyers and sellers. That stuff is way over-rated.

We've had nine recessions since World War II, we've had two presidents shot, one died and one made it, President Reagan. We've had changes in the Supreme Court, we've had changes in Congress, we've had wars. You've had all sorts of things happening since World War II. And the stock market's gone up, you know, over that period of time.

So, trying to predict all these events is just not worth it. Do your work and say 'I believe in the system, I'm going to buy an equity mutual fund' or 'I'm going to have a low-cost index fund, which will just reflect the market index. I don't want to buy a fully managed fund.' That's fine too.

You can do your own research and say, 'I want to participate or I want to do it directly. And I can use some methods that make sense. The same kind of thing I do when I buy an apartment or I buy a second house or I buy a car.' Those methods work in the stock market.

Q: So what did you learn about yourself over the years you were a fund manager?

A: I guess the thing I learned about myself was I looked too much for short-term movements in the stock. My greatest mistakes were things like selling Toys 'R' Us way too early. Stock went up, it was a little bit rich, and a lot of people said Milton Petrie, owner of Petrie Stores, is buying part of Toys 'R' Us and as soon as he bought the last 20%, the theory was the stock would go down. Because he was pushing and pushing and pushing that he was going to own this 20%. Well, guess what, it did go down, it went down 3 or 4 points. And I sold it then, and I forgot to get back in. I got back in later. But, it went up about 20-fold when I waited. I mean, you don't need many of those in your lifetime. You don't want to miss the Home Depots, the McDonald's, the huge stocks—just because temporarily it was a little ahead of itself.

But, Toys 'R' Us is only in maybe a quarter of the country. They still have overseas opportunities. I mean, this was early in the story. You should look at the stock as a baseball game. You ought to say 'What inning am I in?' You want to buy stocks in the first inning if you can. But you can buy them in their second or third inning too. They've got the story right, they've got the balance sheet. They're just going to replicate and roll with it.

You don't want to buy them when it's in the eighth or ninth inning. You have to say, 'How long is this game?' This is a company that can only go into 500 malls; let's say there are 500 first-class malls in the United States. If they're in all 500, where can they go after that?

McDonald's almost ran out. You say to yourself, here's McDonald's, there are only so many they can put in the United States. But, they went overseas. You know, they opened three or four a day overseas. That's what kept McDonald's going for two or three more decades. The stores went and went. That's not so true for retailers. Fast food has gone overseas, but retail has more of a hard time.

Toys 'R' Us has done an okay job. Most retailers, like Limited or Gap, have not been able to go overseas. But, some restaurant chains, particularly fast food, have been able to do it. So, you have to look and say, 'Am I near the end of the story here? I bought this as a cyclical turnaround; this has gotten terrible, to mediocre, to good, to terrific, we're near the peak.' You buy that for maybe a two- or three-year investment. That's a different kind of investment; that's a turnaround.

Well, if you buy in the growth company you say to yourself, 'Is this a 20-, 30-year story—I'm in the third year of it—or is this just going to be so big, they get there very fast and then it's all over and there's no place to go.' You have to say, 'Does this have room to grow?' You have to work that out yourself. You have to say to yourself, 'I think I'm very early in this.' And it becomes like Automatic Data Processing, which had double-digit earnings growth every year for years. All they do is payrolls, that's all they do.

Well, people have only outsourced about 15% of the payrolls in the United States. You might have said 20 years ago, well, this company has done really well, there's no potential. Well, maybe people only outsource 5% of the payrolls. I mean, it's something people don't like to do. It's not a profit center at a company. They say we'll do it for you, we'll do a better job, we'll cut your costs. You have people living in New Hampshire, working in Massachusetts or vice versa and you've got complicated tax situations—who wants to do that stuff? So, they said we'll take over. We'll just do it for you, we'll save you money and be more efficient.

Q: Let's talk a little bit about taking risk in the stock market and how it differs from gambling.

A: I think a lot of people spend a lot of time looking at stocks and looking at charts, and they do a lot of complicated math formulas when they're thinking of buying a stock. You have to understand risk. It's the same kind of risk you have when you play poker, or the same kind of risk when you play bridge. You have to say the odds might favor me in this hand; in bridge maybe there are six spades out against you and you think they're going to split 3 and 3. And guess what, the split is a 6, 0 and you go down. But, that's the way you do it.

You look at your hand in poker and you say if I can draw one card from the deck I still have a losing hand, and you better fold. Or, if you have a terrific hand, a prevailing hand, out of nowhere come four 8s and you lose. But play the hand right, over time, and you'll prevail.

Sometimes luck will just go against you. So, you have to say, if I'm right, how much will I make? If I'm wrong, how much will I lose? If I'm wrong, the stock could lose 30%. If I'm right, I can triple my money. That's a good risk-reward ratio.

One of the worst things to do is say, this company is at 100, and if I'm right they're only going to earn $2 a share, so it's 50 times earnings, and it's not going to grow that much. The stock price is already discounting great things happening. If I'm right I don't think I can make a lot of money. That wouldn't be a good risk-reward ratio. If I'm right, the stock might go up 10%; if I'm wrong, I might lose $50.

You want to find ones that can triple your money if you're right; if you're wrong you might lose 30%, 40%. That's a fair risk to take. And then you have to make sure the story is getting better. You just don't play stocks like the lottery. You say, this is the risk/reward, and the story is getting better. And if you're wrong and the story slips, you say okay, I made a mistake.

Q: So, everybody has to learn bridge or poker.

A: I think bridge or poker would be very useful for investors.

Q: Can you define for us the efficient market theory and tell me whether you agree with it?

A: Well, efficient market theory says all the things about a company are discounted. That investors already know all the good or bad news about a stock. The market knows the stock's gone up because it means things look terrific, the stock's gone down means things are terrible. So, what's happening is this information is being discounted all the time. That's the popular theory; you can't beat that.

But, the equation is people forget about companies. They've done poorly for awhile, but then they start to turn around and people forget to look at them, forget to analyze it. They just lose interest in them, they hate them.

Or, vice versa: companies go up and their stocks are doing well, people get sort of complacent and they stop analyzing, and they start saying this is a great company, it's the best thing you've ever seen. And guess what? Competitors come along or one of the new parts doesn't work, or they saturate a market.

So, I think normally if you look at ten stocks, there are what I call new-high risks. These are companies doing well. There's a reason for it. Probably nine times out of ten they're great stories. Maybe one time out of ten, you should say wait a second, this story isn't so hot anymore. It's starting to slip.

If you look at ten stocks doing poorly, nine of them probably are genuine losers. There's a reason the stock went down. And maybe one out of ten times you'll find something—boy this company has a good balance sheet, they're getting better, one of their competitors just went under, they have a new product. Normally I'd say nine out of ten times stocks are efficiently priced. It's that one time out of ten where you have an opportunity. So, more times, the more stocks you look at the more chances you have to find a winner.

Q: What do you think your biggest contribution will be to the investing public? What will you be remembered for?

A: Well, I hope people will be careful with their money. I mean, people are generally very careful with everything they do. I mean, they'll spend three hours trying to save $150 on a round-trip air ticket to California. People do not ordinarily spend money in a stupid way. But for some reason, they'll hear a tip on a stock on a bus or at a dinner party, and they'll put half their life's savings in it before the next sunset. I mean, that doesn't work.

So, I'm trying to teach people to either do it right or don't do it at all.

When you own a stock, you own a piece of a company. It's not a lottery ticket. The company does well, the stock does well. It's not a gamble, it's not a bet. You're investing in a company, you're part owner. You own bonds in that company, at maturity they just give you back your money and say thank you very much, and they pay interest. But, if you own shares in the company, you participate.

If you had held McDonald's bonds for the last 30 years the company would have said thank you very much, and paid you the interest rate. At maturity they'd give you back your money. If you owned the stock you would have made 50, 100 times your money. You shared in it. That's why you own stocks, you're an owner.

Q: So, don't listen to all the noise.

A: Don't listen to noise. Cut out the noise. Noise is not useful. Look at facts instead. If you own an auto company, you ought to care what's happening to used-car prices, you ought to care what's happening to steel prices, you ought to care what's happening to affordability. What's happening to new cars coming in from Europe, new cars coming from Asia? That's what you ought to be looking at, not worrying about who's going to be the next president and what's happening in Congress, what's happening in the Supreme Court, what's happening in the Middle East. Those are things you have no control over.

I would love to know what the stock market is going to do next year; that would be useful stuff. I'd love to know what's going to happen with interest rates. I'd love to have a great crystal ball. No one has one.

What you can do is individual company analysis and say this company looks like they have it, and I'm going to keep monitoring it. As long as they're doing well, I'm going to hang in there. When the story or the fundamentals slip, I'm going to say bye-bye.

Q: Peter, what have both your hits and your misses had in common?

A: Well, I'd say normally I've bought some long shots. I've probably batted two hundred, two hundred fifty in my career. But on long shots, I think I'm 0 for 25. I've never made money. These are companies that have amazing products, sound terrific, or they're going to earn $800 a share if the new product works.

Well, guess what, they don't have it yet, it's an idea. It's all sizzle, no steak. Those haven't worked.

But I've had stocks like Stop 'n' Shop. I thought I might make a third, I might make 40% on my money. And guess what? They rolled out Bradlees stores all over the Northeast and then they came up with Super Stop 'n' Shop. It was an enormous stock, and it went up fifteen- to twentyfold. It surprised me; it took a lot of years to do that. I look back and say, 'Wow, look how much money I made in this, look at how much money I made in Dunkin' Donuts, look at how much money I made in Taco Bell.'

I didn't expect it when I bought it. They were good companies, they were doing well. The stories stayed intact, in some cases got better. The same with Fannie Mae, Chrysler. They just kept getting better, and I didn't expect it.

So I've been lucky enough to have some stocks that went up ten-, twentyfold. They were surprises. The ones where I said: 'Wow! If this works I'm going to make twentyfold, I've never broken even. I'm 0 for 20.'

Long shots are no shots. And if you have a stock that's really exciting, a great story but no earnings and no sales and the stock's $4, it's OK to tune in later. If it's going to $300, it's OK to buy it at $8, it's OK to buy it at $12. Tune in later, see if it's for real. Normally you find out there's no quote on it and it's gonzo. Don't try those guys.

Q: What do you think about U.S. companies' competitiveness in the global economy? How competitive do you believe American corporations are today?

A: I think there's been a big argument the last five, ten years, about how bad American industry is. This is amazing, when you think that Boeing is the best at what it does, John Deere's the best at what it does, Caterpillar Tractor is the best at what it does, Harley-Davidson's the best at what it does. We lead the world in biotechnology. Software is about a ninety-five percent American industry. Personal computers. Intel, Microsoft are the best. It just goes on and on.

The most important machine invented in the automobile industry didn't come from Canada, didn't come from Japan, didn't come from Germany, it came from Detroit. This was Chrysler inventing the minivan. Our steel industry's gotten better, our copper industry's gotten better, our paper industry's improved, our porous plastic industry got better. We're doing well in telecommunications and networking.

American industry is doing a terrific job, we're really turned it around. And somehow we've had this idea that we're inept. It's not true.

Q: So, the sky is the limit?

A: No. We have to continue to invent. We've had 3,000 companies come public in the last four years. This has provided a lot of money for working capital, research and development, new equipment. Three thousand companies. There's only 3,000 companies on the entire New York Stock Exchange. But 3,000 companies is a lot. That's two each business day.

In the last four years in Europe, only 125 companies have come public. I don't think 3,000 companies have become public in Europe since Charlemagne, and I think he became king of the Franks in 768. I mean, this is a very big thing for our country. This is not just rich people getting rich, this is money that creates productivity, jobs. We've added 15 million jobs in American in the last 30 years. Europe—which is larger than we are—has only added six million new jobs. The U.K.'s added no jobs in the last 30 years. Jobs have gone down in Europe in 1991, '92, '93, '94, '95. They went up a little bit in '96. They've had a down decade for jobs.

We added 18 million jobs in the 1980s. The five largest companies eliminated three million jobs. But we added 18 million—these are small and medium-sized businesses: Federal Express started out and did really well. Compaq Computer, Staples started in Boston with one store in Brighton, now it's a $20 billion industry. MCI has done very well, Federal Express has done well. Federal Express has made the post office more efficient. MCI has made telecommunication costs go down. They all have done well, that's helped everybody. No one loses in that.

These are companies that make a difference. So this is what's made our country great, these small and medium-sized enterprises. All you ever hear about is big companies laying people off. You'd think no one's working in America. The European Union is a third bigger than the United States. They've added six million jobs in the last eight years, we've added fifty.

I mean, who's doing a better job? We are. And this investing, this going public, it's a great thing for our country, it's a fantastic thing for jobs, for everybody. Everybody wins. This is not a zero-sum game. When companies do well, everybody does well.

Q: Your latest book is called *Learn to Earn.* Tell me about it.

A: Well, this is a book I wrote with John Rothchild. I think it's useful for younger people or people that've never looked at stocks, never looked at bonds, who don't understand business, don't understand savings. They could be 25, 35, 65, they're a chemistry professor, they're a teacher, they know nothing about the stock market. You ought to learn something. It's sad today. You learn a lot of things in school. You don't know what a bond is, you don't learn about savings, you don't learn about the stock market. There's no courses in high school. There's games, but there's no courses. You could spend your whole life and not know why bonds go up or down. Instead they teach cosine. I haven't used cosine in the last 20 years.

So I tried to give the basics: what business is about, what savings is about, why people have done well in the market, why they haven't. It's really a general philosophy of how you can start this exercise. It's a primer, it's a start.

Q: In your last chapter, toward the end of the book, you talk about heroes. What makes a hero?

A: Well, a person that starts a business is a hero. That's what's made America go. Somebody had to start General Electric, somebody had to start Eastman Kodak. People that start businesses take a lot of risks. There were 1.5 million businesses started in the 1980s. Even if each one had just ten employees, that's fifteen million jobs. Some didn't make it.

We never hear about this. All we ever hear about is big companies letting people go: downsizing, rightsizing, reengineering—whatever gerund you want to use. But you never hear about the companies that are starting. Medium-sized companies are growing to large-size companies, small companies grow to be medium-sized. That's what makes our country go. We need it. Those are my idea of America's heroes.

CHAPTER FOUR

PLEASANT ROWLAND

FOUNDER
AND PRESIDENT,
PLEASANT COMPANY

❯ ❯ ❯

PLEASANT ROWLAND

FOUNDER
AND PRESIDENT,
PLEASANT COMPANY

When one first hears Pleasant Rowland's tale, one is almost tempted to warn others against trying to emulate her success. Don't attempt this at home, in other words. Then it becomes clear that Rowland can indeed be emulated, that her experience can inspire. She performed one of the most basic business feats: She saw a need and met it. Saw a void and filled it, with an outfit she called Pleasant Company.

Rowland's story begins at Christmastime in 1983. She was looking for some special gifts to give to her nieces, dolls specifically. As it turns out, she was particularly disappointed with her options. "That was the year that Cabbage Patch hit the market with such a phenomenon. And all my choices that year for Christmas presents were Cabbage Patch dolls and Barbie."

It was her surprise and disappointment in those limited selections that started her thinking about the sorry state of affairs in the toy business. "Neither of my choices were particularly pretty and I didn't think they were of a very high quality. But most important, they didn't say anything about what it meant to be a girl growing up in America. And they weren't something I thought anybody was going to treasure." Rowland thought to herself: Can I be the only woman looking for dolls this Christmas and feeling disappointed in my options?

What Rowland didn't realize was that at that moment, she stood at a crossroads. Then, in 1985, Rowland first conceived of Pleasant Company—a concept that combined her love of American history with a commitment to educational products. "It was an idea of books and dolls that would bring history alive," Rowland says, "that would provide girls with role models, showing that the essentials of growing up haven't changed very much, in spite of the differences in the world in the last two hundred and fifty years."

To achieve her goal, Rowland basically broke most of the rules that are chiseled in stone on the walls of the marketing hall of fame. She had no experience in the business she was about to tackle, she invested her entire life savings in the idea, she had no money for advertising and she conducted no focus groups. Nor did she ever set a financial goal for the company.

Not surprisingly, she hit brick walls when she proposed her idea to bankers and investors. Rowland recalls that very few people at the time believed her idea could come to fruition. "Men just didn't understand it, didn't think the dolls were necessary. They couldn't understand the subtlety of a different message that we were trying to send. They were complimentary, but there was not a real 'taking seriously' that this could ever amount to anything."

One of the early disbelievers still stands out in Rowland's memory. "I remember relating my idea to a very successful entrepreneur. He listened, and at the end of our lunch, he said, "Pleasant, it sounds like you want to start General Motors. You're talking about the direct mail business, you're talking about the publishing business, you're talking about special events, you're talking about entertainment, you're talking about being in the doll business, the book business, the clothing business. Get real!"

Rowland got real all right. A little over ten years later she presides over an immensely profitable—and real—doll, clothing, publishing, empire. It may not have the revenues of General Motors, but it is the Cadillac of the doll business.

Nothing about this success was easy. "Necessity is the mother of invention," she quips. "I was going up against the major toy companies in America. It was very very hard to imagine how I was going to get shelf space in Toys 'R' Us or Wal-Mart. I certainly couldn't afford television advertising. Those were all great blessings in disguise."

But don't let anyone tell you little girls are easy to please. Says Rowland: "Children are very, very smart consumers. They know what they want. I think they care dearly about these dolls. They take good care of them, they play with them hard. They cherish them and they know that they have got something that's important. It's not just another thing. They have their buckets of Barbies, but then they have their American Girl doll."

Today, Pleasant Rowland is hailed as a pioneer of the girls' market, yet the core products she is selling, books and dolls, have been the staples of girlhood for centuries. Rowland says simply that she took the old favorites and put "vitamins in the chocolate cake." The vitamins? Unlikely as it may seem, American history. The books in The American Girls Collection bring American history alive through the eyes of five 9-year-old heroines living at different times in America's past. Dolls of these heroines with historically accurate clothing and miniature accessories are now cherished possessions for girls aged 7 to 12.

Rowland expanded her brand in 1993 to address the issues of girls growing up today. Using the same formula, she created *American Girl* magazine, which now has 670,000 subscribers. She added the American Girl of Today dolls, their clothing and accessories, as well as a line of girls' clothing called American Girl Gear. Rowland still distributes her products almost exclusively by direct mail, with some added help for her books from wide bookstore distribution throughout the country. She mails almost 40 million catalogs a year and has sold more than 40 million books and more than 3 million dolls. In just a decade, Pleasant Company is more than a $250 million enterprise.

Here's how she did it.

❦ ❦ ❦

Q: Pleasant, was there some aspect of your childhood that you were trying to re-create when you started Pleasant Company?

A: I had a happy childhood, and it was a time when family life was simpler. I loved to read as a little girl. I can remember discovering the books in my grandmother's second-floor bookshelf that my dad had had when he was little. I discovered the Oz books there. I remember just delving into them, barely moving for days at a time, flung across my bed. I was an avid reader. And I had three sisters. We played with our dolls. It was just a simpler time. I loved it.

Life has gotten a lot more complicated. So the real inspiration for The American Girl's Collection came somewhere from that childhood experience. But it really came into clear focus for me one Christmas when I was trying to buy dolls for my nieces.

Q: Describe that situation.

A: I had gone Christmas shopping for my nieces, who were about eight and ten years old at the time I think. I wanted to give them something to remember Aunt Pleasant with and something that they might give to their daughters and pass on from generation to generation. That was the year that Cabbage Patch hit the market with such a phenomenon. All my choices that year for Christmas presents were Cabbage Patch dolls and Barbie dolls. I just felt that neither was what I wanted to give. I didn't think they were particularly pretty and I didn't think they were of a very high quality. But most important, they didn't say anything about what it meant to be a girl growing up in America. And they weren't something I thought anybody was going to treasure and put away for their own daughters.

I thought, 'I can't be the only woman looking for attractive, high-quality dolls this Christmas and disappointed in my options.' So, I think the seed of Pleasant Company was planted there. But Pleasant Company is the coming together of lots of avenues of my life.

I started my career teaching kindergarten through third grade. I became a television news reporter in San Francisco for a short stint, and then had a wonderful opportunity to create textbooks, teaching children to read and write. I loved that part of my career. I did it for ten years, creating the first reading program for kindergarten children. Prior to that, kindergarten had been sort of block corner and doll play, and I thought that kids at that age were really ready to learn. So I wrote my first program in 1970, and spent a decade writing textbooks, still used in schools today. There I fell in love, moved to Wisconsin, and that's a far distance from the publishing industry in Boston where I had been working. When I got to Wisconsin I was looking for something that could really use me. I had done my thing in publishing, I had done teaching.

Then my husband went to a convention at Colonial Williamsburg. I went along and was just blown away by that experience. History and American traditions truly came alive there for me. I loved the entire experience of walking in the footsteps of that colonial world. I realized we have not done a good job bringing history alive for kids in schools. And I had spent a decade working on reading instructional materials, so I knew what there was. I thought, isn't there some way that I can make the magic of this historic place come alive for little girls? And the following Christmas was the Cabbage Patch/Barbie experience.

Somewhere in the midst of all of that, The American Girl's Collection was born: books and dolls that would bring history alive and that would provide girls with role models. I wanted to show that the real essentials of growing up haven't changed very much, in spite of the differences in the world in the last two hundred and fifty years. And so the characters of The American Girl's Collection were designed to be good role models for girls. I think that girls imagine those lives and see models of creativity and determination and courage and kindness and spunkiness and bravery. And they are not extreme. These are not bigger-than-life heroines. These are real little girls dealing with the problems of growing as little girls.

The dolls bring the entire experience alive. And, while the dolls are the first thing that most people think of when they think of Pleasant Company, it's really not all I think this company is about. But I do believe that the dolls give girls the opportunity to play out those stories of history.

Q: In addition to the dolls, you publish *American Girl Magazine*—which has a circulation of almost 700,000. And you also have the American Girl Library and the American Girl Collection books, which have sold 36 million copies. You have sold over 3 million dolls. Your annual revenues exceed $250 million. Obviously, Pleasant Company is a huge marketing success. What have you done differently in marketing your products, the dolls, the books, everything? What have you done differently that you think has created your success?

A: First of all, I don't think I'm in the doll business or the book business or the direct mail business. I'm in the little girl business. And anything that can make this fragile time of a girl's childhood—between the ages of seven and twelve—better, is something that I think we have a responsibility to do under the purview of this company's mission. So, I didn't define Pleasant Company narrowly, and I think that's very important. Second, you know that necessity is the mother of invention. You must remember, ten years ago when we started, I was up against the giants of Mattel and Hasbro and the major toy companies of America. It was very, very hard to imagine how I was going to get shelf space in Toys 'R' Us or Wal-Mart. I certainly couldn't afford television advertising. And I didn't think for a minute I could stand up against the great toy merchants out there.

As it turned out, those obstacles were all great blessings in disguise. They forced me to think about telling our story in a different way. This was in the early years of the direct mail industry. My own background in publishing had given me great comfort with putting images and words on paper.

I felt comfortable in the catalog medium. Beyond which, The American Girl story is a softer story, a subtler story, and I wanted it told in a softer voice. I didn't think Toys 'R' Us was the right place to tell the story. Catalog marketing was a perfect fit for me. I could really talk to my audience of little girls and their moms and aunts and grandmas and dads. I could tell a story to them even if they never owned a doll, or never bought a book. I was putting something in their hands that in itself was valuable and fun to read and taught its own lessons. I think that catalog marketing was the great match of advertising medium to product. Serendipitous, I suppose, more than anything.

I wrote all of the copy for the original catalog, and did for a long, long time. Talking directly to my audience has been very important. This is a tough world today—a cynical world, vulgar world, full of a lot of tawdry and violent images for kids. We wanted to be something different. I think that's what I'm proudest of doing—that we stayed true to our course. We started from a different set of values and we held true to those values. The great joy of finding this enormous audience hungry for our values, our quality, our perspective on girlhood has been very, very heartening. Way beyond what I ever dreamed of.

Q: Speaking of what you dreamed, along the way there must have been some moments where a wrong turn could have meant disaster. Where, if you had made the wrong decision, you would not be where you are today. Can you recall any points in time along the way in the past ten years that were really pivotal, that were turning points for you?

A: I think there were a couple of key decisions that we made that mattered. Some were things we decided not to do. For example, early on people saw the entertainment opportunity from these stories. The stories are dearly loved by girls. They are beautiful pieces of historical fiction, which would make great films. We have a file a foot thick of wonderful producers who have asked for the film rights to The American Girl's Collection. But we haven't done that. I was so worried that film would make our idea burn with a white hot flame, become a fad, burn out, and go away. I had invested my life savings to start the business. I had cared deeply about its mission, and I didn't want it to be a flash in the pan. I really wanted to stay a long course, to become a classic. So, though it would have been easy to take that money and kind of a rush to have the glamour of the entertainment world, we really eschewed that, and did not follow that course. That was an important decision.

Q: Has the fact that you don't have a business degree contributed to your success?

A: I don't know. I do know I found a lot of very, very dedicated people to work with me. About 80 percent of our employees are women. That is not by design. But I have to say, they are the only people who believed in the beginning that this could ever happen. Men just didn't understand the idea of the products, didn't think that they were necessary, couldn't understand the subtlety of the different message that we were trying to send.

Q: And when you say men didn't understand it, are you talking about bankers that you were trying to get financial help from? Or was it people that you just spoke to in the everyday course of life? How did you get that reading?

A: All of the above. You know, men were complimentary, but there was not a real 'taking seriously' that this idea could really ever amount to anything. Once we started to make money, they were dying to come work here. They could see that it was successful. But being a company for women wasn't the purpose. Being for girls was the purpose, and it still is the purpose.

Q: Your father was an executive in an advertising agency in Chicago; he obviously understood marketing. Do you think you inherited some of this talent? Was there ever talk at the dinner table?

A: Oh, indeed. Dad never lived to see the success of Pleasant Company. But, he probably was my teacher. I loved it when he would come home before presentations to Pillsbury or Green Giant. He would bring home huge portfolios of the advertising presentations and show them to us. I can remember the Campbell's kids, the Marlboro man. He would always talk at dinner about the things that had happened at those presentations. One lesson he taught indirectly, though constantly. He was on the client side of the business, but he had terrific respect for the creative people. He always said, 'Great advertising is created in the detail.' I think that's what I took away. Pleasant Company is a business that I have nurtured in every detail.

Q: It is clear that details count at Pleasant Company, right down to the tiny little needlepoint one of the dolls is doing. The microscopic detail is pretty amazing.

A: But I think that's what *I* would have adored as a child. You know, we didn't do any market research in the beginning, at all. That's how gut-driven this company is.

Q: You basically broke the rules?

A: In the area of market research, we did. You know, I was creating a product that I would have loved when I was eight years old. I was the test. There was exactly one focus group. I'll tell you the focus group story. Someone said, 'You know, you really shouldn't go off and launch all of this without doing focus groups.' So we went to Chicago and we had the fancy focus groups, and hired the person to lead them, and had some sample products.

Q: Were the participants mothers or daughters or both?

A: They were mothers. 'Would anyone buy these products?' was the question on the table. For the first 45 minutes of the focus group it was dreadful. The group hated everything about The American Girl Collection because we were merely talking about the idea as a concept. Then we brought out the products. It was a 180-degree turn. I learned a great lesson. Forget the focus group. Go do what you believe you're going to go do. Come from a place of heart. Come from a place of mission. There will be people out there who will love this and admire it, if you love it and admire it.

So, the whole criterion for developing our products for a long, long time—longer than most people would ever have believed and still a huge part of it today—is, 'Do I, Pleasant Rowland, like it?' 'Would I have liked it when I was eight years old?' And if the answer is 'yes,' we make it. Bottom line, if I think it should be pink, it's pink.

Q: Let's talk a little bit about creativity, which is very important as a marketer. Do you think this is something you can learn, or is it innate? How can you be creative? How can you do that as a marketer?

A: I think these are my gifts. I can't give you any answer to 'Where ideas come from.' I don't know where ideas come from. I don't know why I'm the one who got this idea and other smart people in the world didn't. This business for girls is what I believe I was meant to do with my life. You know, there was one other thing I'd like to tell you about my dad. He had a little 3 × 5 card tucked in the corner of his mirror. It said, and I can't remember it exactly, but the essence of it was, that what you should want for life is an arena big enough to express your talents and gifts. Pleasant Company is that arena. I have been blessed with enormous opportunities and enormous gifts. They all come together here for me. I love coming to work. I love what we do here at Pleasant Company. I love the difference we make. It allows me to write. It allows me to create. It allows me to lead. It allows me to be surrounded by smart people that nourish me, and I hope I nourish them. It's a very yeasty, fulfilling environment to be a part of.

Q: You're a great communicator. How important is it for you to keep communicating with your audience, with your customers, with your potential customers? You must get letters galore.

A: We do, and now we get e-mail galore. We have a Web site, which is great fun. It's so instantaneous, we get to hear what girls think and want. That's the feedback. That's our fuel. One of the disadvantages of a direct mail business is that you don't have hands-on experience with your customers. Where, if you own a store, you can see them come in and 'Ooh' and 'Ah' and get excited. I think our phone operators, frankly, have the best job at Pleasant Company. They get to have the direct contact with our customers. I get a fix of it every Christmas. I go in for a few days every year and take phone calls. No one ever realizes that it's me on the phone. And I say, 'Good Morning, Pleasant

Company. This is Pleasant.' And they just zoom right on into the conversation! I think the feedback we get in the form of letters from girls and parents is extraordinary. But, you know, people talk with their purses, and let's not forget this. The fact that we have customers who are as loyal as they are for as long as they are, who understand what our values are about providing an alternative, about taste and about judgment, those are the people who really keep this company going. They're the ones who feed us and encourage us to keep doing the kind of quality work we do.

Q: Now Pleasant Company is getting a little competition, because you are so successful. Are you going to change the way you run your business, the way you market your products to respond to the competition that's coming into the marketplace?

A: You can spend your life looking over your shoulder, or you can spend your life looking ahead. We're going to look ahead. We have lots of wonderful ideas that we want to bring to girls. Wonderful things that we can do and should do as the leader in the market of products for girls in this age group. People trust us. We've established faith with our customers, and gained the affection of their daughters. I don't think we're going to change.

Q: You dealt with tough competition from the very beginning. As you pointed out, you had Mattel and Hasbro and all of the major toy companies to go up against. But you did really find yourself a niche. And you've filled it beautifully and now people are trying to pile in.

A: But they don't come from the same place that we do. They want a piece of the market. That's not what motivates this company. I think they want to be in the doll business or they want to be in the book business. We really are coming from a very different definition. We are in the girl business. We're here to make a difference in those lives. If the competition does good quality products, then there is more good stuff out there for girls. I think that's really fine, and I mean that very genuinely. There was an enormous void of quality products for girls a decade ago when I started this company. We have filled it with a successful company that makes good quality products. If that motivates other people, terrific. If we've raised the quality bar, terrific. That just means there is more good products and more quality programming. I think it's all for the good of this world. I'm not worried. There are a lot of girls out there. We're not going to have everything that every little girl wants. We come from a place of heart and mission that is important to us. I think it's good if there are other people who fill that niche.

Q: In talking with your customers, has there been any one story that you found to be most rewarding about how you affected a girl somewhere?

A: There really are legions of them. Every fall we have a company kickoff, because, as you can imagine, we're in the Santa Claus business in a big way here. We have about 3,000 employees who come in to help us fulfill our orders for Santa Claus. One of the things that's so important to me and to the other employees who are here all year long is that these people feel the same sense of urgency and mission that the rest of us feel. So, we have a fall kickoff every year, usually on the loading dock, where we can get the most chairs. I always try to find one letter we've received that year to read aloud. One that I remember was written by a little Amish girl who wanted a doll. The family was poor and couldn't afford it. So, she raised a pig. She took the pig to the county fair, won a blue ribbon, and sold the pig. With the proceeds, she bought a Kirsten doll. That delights me.

People think this is a rich girl's product. It's not. There are little girls who save very, very hard and treasure what they get. You know, I think children are very, very smart consumers, in truth. They know what they want. Vis-à-vis the competition. You know, no one who wants a Barbie is going to accept a generic plastic doll as Barbie. Nobody who wants Nike shoes is going to accept anything else. Little girls want a real American Girl doll. The imitators aren't the real thing. I know that girls care dearly about these dolls. They take good care of them, they play with them hard. They cherish them, and they know that they have got something that's important. It's not just another 'thing.' They have their buckets of Barbies, but then they have their one special American Girl doll.

Q: You've taken a great idea and extended it into a variety of different areas—the magazines, the books, museums. Could you tell me how you decide what to pursue? How do you know that you're not going to reach a saturation point?

A: Let me speak first about one interesting thing that you have raised, which is the museum program and our special events. The motivation for all of that was the realization that girls and their moms don't have many meaningful experiences together. They go to the mall or they go shopping. But, in truth, where dads tend to have camping and hiking or sports in common with their sons, mothers and daughters don't have many memorable things that they could do. When I was a little girl, my mother once took me to hear the Chicago Symphony. I remember that day like it was yesterday. It was so special that it was just me—not my sisters, just me—and just the two of us had gone downtown to do something that seemed very grown up and very special. It is a wonderful memory that I have carried with me for a long time. So, that's part of my childhood I wanted to try to find a way to give back.

Our special events division was designed to create memorable moments and memories of them. We partner with non-profit organizations around the country that benefit children's charities. We provide them with fund-raising events: The American Girls' Fashion Shows, Samantha's Ice Cream Social. The non-profit organizations invite mothers and daughters and grandmas and aunts to come. The proceeds of these events all go to charity. This is a nonprofit effort for Pleasant Company. Last year we raised two million dollars for children's charities. But, you know, this is a marketing tool, as well. It allows our products to get in front of girls and their parents. To be seen first hand, where in a catalog all they can see is a picture. I think the experience that takes place at those events is a very, very meaningful experience for girls and their moms to share. We've done a lot of good at the same time, we've continued to market our product.

As for reaching the saturation point, we're careful about that. We starve our customers a little bit for new products. It takes two years for us to introduce a new character to the market. We introduce three book episodes in one year and then three the next. We have had to grow within our means. So, we haven't perhaps done the obvious things and have done the less obvious things, because they were opportunities that nobody was taking advantage of. That's sort of the story of the whole business. This was a market niche that now we're being called the pioneers of. I guess that's really true. There wasn't much in the marketplace for girls of this age ten years ago. Now people have said, 'Oh, wow! Something's going on there!' and started to add products to it. We are thoughtful about the products we introduce. We don't want to oversaturate. I don't think we have. One of the pluses we have is that when you serve a children's market, it's an evergreen market meaning that there are always new kids entering our age group for whom the American Girls are a first-time experience.

So, we have a new audience every year, as well as the tried-and-true who have been with us for four and five years. The American Girl of Today, which was introduced a year ago, is an opportunity for us to go in a different direction.

Q: Explain what that is.

A: We introduced the American Girl of Today in 1995. Up until that point our product line had been focused on the five historical characters. We began to see that there was a whole raft of issues that girls of today were dealing with that we couldn't get at in historical fiction. So, we created *American Girl* magazine as a way of talking to girls about those issues in their lives today. We feel we've set role models in place with the characters from the past. Now we want today's girls to see that they're part of history too. That this is their moment and their issues and their lives are important. They are the heroines of their own story. I think by creating the American Girl of Today, we have opened many, many opportunities that perhaps we didn't have with just the historical characters. Out of the contemporary concept we have developed American Girl Gear, which is a line of girl's clothing.

I think it's very important to do this. Girls of this age become very body conscious and very self-conscious. Self image is formed during these very important years. How they dress is—as all women know for their whole lives—a statement of who they are. We didn't want girls looking like little Madonna wannabes at ten. Yet we wanted them to have clothing that felt fun and with-it and of today. We have also created American Girl Library, a wonderful series of advice and activity books that we introduced last year. It's a very, very big success. Each title sold over a hundred thousand in its introductory season last Christmas. Again this series is about issues that girls face. Friendship, family issues, advice about all the peer issues that girls have. Pleasant Company's products appeal to girls over a long, long range of ages.

Girls typically come to the product line around age seven. And they stay engrossed usually till about 13 or 14. And the historical characters are of particular interest up in the early years of that development cycle, from ages seven to eleven. Then girls begin to leave their fantasy worlds behind and become more engrossed in their peers and in the world around them.

This is when Girl of Today clicks in. The *American Girl* magazine is very popular with these girls as they get older—from fourth grade up. We feel we've extended our line to deal with the issues that girls of today deal with.

We have done no international marketing yet. We think there really is an opportunity for us. But we have picked our way carefully among the options, through the thicket of American mass culture. Mostly, we've tried to go where there isn't a lot of competition.

Q: Pleasant, if you were to teach Pleasant Company as a case in business school, what would you say about it? How would the interested observer view this success?

A: I don't really know what it is that's transferable to somebody else's business. Certainly there's one very obvious thing we did. We were really the first people to take this audience of girls seven to twelve seriously. Perhaps that's the ripple effect of the women's movement. My colleagues and I were products of the last twenty years of progress that women have made. We realized that our daughters were going to be affected by the world around them, and we didn't like what we were seeing for them in the world.

Then I think we just broke a lot of rules because we didn't know the rules. If I'd had an MBA I suppose I would have done things a lot differently. I probably would have listened to that focus group a lot harder. And I probably wouldn't have believed I could have done it.

I remember one time I sat with a man who was a very successful entrepreneur, and I told him my idea, and he listened, and at the end of the lunch he said, 'Pleasant, it sounds like you want to start General Motors.' And I said, 'No, I just want to do all these things for girls.' He said, 'But those are all different businesses. You're talking about the direct mail business, you're talking about the publishing business, you're talking about special events, you're talking about a form of entertainment, you're talking about being in the doll business, the book business, the clothing business. Get real!'

I think I had all these goals because I'd never been in business. I didn't know this was supposed to be so hard. I don't mean to be naive and I don't mean to be simplistic, but I just wanted to do it.

So at the root, it comes from a place of real passion. I care a whole lot about this mission, this business of serving girls. And I cared a lot ten years ago. So passion is incredibly important. And I think most entrepreneurs and most people starting businesses don't have the wherewithal to go up against the giants.

Look for a different way to do it. We did find different ways. But most important, we listened to our own hearts. We wanted to reach this audience and really talk to them.

The world doesn't need more 'stuff.' I guess if I were to talk to anybody, I would say make sure that what you're doing is either so much better, or so different that it really does fill a void. We filled a void. I think our competition today isn't filling the void, they're just adding more of the same. I think they're a little bit cookie-cutter. We became the pioneer because we filled a real void. But you know, in the beginning, ignorance is bliss. If I'd ever known what I was undertaking, perhaps I would have gotten cold feet.

Q: And was there ever a moment when you were downcast or when there had been a hurdle that you couldn't jump? Was there ever a moment when you felt that you just can't go on, that it's just not going to work?

A: No. I never dreamed Pleasant Company would be as successful as it is. I never quantified it. We did have a business plan. It was a three-year business plan, I think. And we beat it pretty good in the first couple of years, so the numbers didn't hold. But we stayed very true to the course of that plan.

There were tough times. What I remember, though, were the good times. I remember the wonderful people who happened in my way. What did I know about the doll business? What did I know?

Q: So how did you go about finding it?

A: At the beginning, I had one other person working with me. Her name was Sue Weston. I said, 'Sue, go to Chicago and find a cute doll. Antique store, department store, find us some cute dolls, because we've got to have something as the initial aesthetic vocabulary to start from.'

She called me the first day and said, 'Pleasant, I thought this was going to be a no-brainer. This is really hard. The dolls that are available are hideous.' I said, 'That's why we're starting this business. Find something.' She stayed in Chicago another day. Then she called me and said, 'I'm coming home, I have something.' But she said, 'I don't think you're going to think this doll is too cute.' I said, 'What's wrong?' She said, 'The eyes are crossed and it had been sitting on the shelf in the back room at Marshall Field's for a long time. The buyer didn't even know where it had come from. But I have it and I hope you'll think it's cute.' As a matter of fact, it was.

But the doll had no label, no box, no nothing. Now we knew someone in the world made a cute doll, but we didn't know who or where the person was. We undressed the doll, and stitched into its underpants was a little label that said Götz Puppenfabrik, Rodenthal, Germany. We called long distance to Rodenthal and got so caught up in the rush of trying to locate Götz Puppenfabrik that we did not realize that 6 o'clock at night in Madison, Wisconsin was one in the morning in Rodenthal, Germany. A sleepy voice answered the phone in German and I suddenly froze, realizing that I had awakened some poor soul in the middle of the night. With that my one year of college German went completely out of my mind.

We had a very brief conversation, in which I established who they were and got an address. Then I wrote them a letter asking if they would custom make our dolls. The Götz family are wonderful people. Here they were half a world away, and they believed in me when *nobody* should have believed in me. What did I know about the toy business? And they agreed to make our first thousand dolls.

I had to guarantee the purchase order personally. Then there was the young man in China, twenty-one years old who was working for his dad. They were making stuffed animals. His name is Jonathan So. We were looking for people to make doll clothes. Minimum orders in the Far East are so huge, nobody would talk to us. But Jonathan said, 'Okay, I'll make some for you when my father's factory isn't busy.' Today Jonathan So has an enormous factory in China. He is hugely successful. He has stayed with us as the Götz family in Germany has stayed with us. And we have a family of vendors that have really supported us through this phenomenal growth. That's very unusual to find partners who are able to grow with you. We quickly outgrew the Mom and Pop shops, and we outgrew the Aunt and Uncle shops. Finally we are able now to go anywhere in the world to buy our product. But we came across some wonderful people in the process. I believe they were put in my path.

Q: You didn't find them? They found you?

A: It's both. There isn't a single successful person out there who will not attribute a very big piece of their life to luck. The idea of a company to serve girls was an idea whose time had come. I was a very, very determined individual doing the very best I could to bring it to life. But I had some enormous good fortune with the people that I came upon in the course of building this business.

Q: Describe the corporate culture here at Pleasant Company. It's very different.

A: It is really a culture informed by mission. I think you could go to the shipping docks, and the man who loads the truck could tell you what the mission of this company is. I know it sounds a little Goody Two-shoes in a very cynical world, but we think what we do here is important, and we think it's important to do it well. There is an aura of quality and perfectionism about this place, perhaps because a lot of us are women.

Perhaps it's because I, the owner, am a woman. We take a huge pride in having made a difference, and we want to keep making that difference. If the competition can match us, then the world is better for having more good stuff for girls, but in the meantime we're going to do our thing as well as we can. There are fabulous people here who work awfully hard to make that happen.

Q: What would you describe as your strengths and weaknesses? You've already said that you don't have an MBA, that you don't know the book on marketing, that you didn't know what you were doing. Still, what were your strengths and what were your weaknesses along the way?

A: You know our vices are the excesses of our virtues. I'm determined, I'm quick, I'm creative, I process very fast. I like to think out of the box. I think I'm hard to work for, for all of those reasons. I don't suffer fools gladly. I think I've gotten better about this, but I'm still not as good as I should be. I'm impatient with mediocrity. It's one thing to be impatient and try to do something about it, and it's another thing to be impatient and just have people think you're impatient. So I work at that, too.

I am very determined. And I suppose if you get in my way and don't understand how important this business and mission are to me, you're going to think I'm brusque and tough and unfeeling. It's because I think what I do here is important and I do it with a real sense of urgency. 'Let's get on with it,' is my attitude. That's what motivates the company, but I don't think that makes me easy to work for.

I think the people here who love to work for Pleasant Rowland, are the people on the operations end. Because I love learning about what they do. I'm a student to them. I don't know how to run the catalog business or a publishing company as well as they do. I don't know how to do many of the wonderful things that happen here. For instance, how we import from all over the world and get it here on time. The people with those jobs have great autonomy. The people who probably have a harder time working for me are the people on the creative end of the business. We create all our own catalogs, all our own advertising, all our point-of-purchase displays in house. All of our design work happens here. We produce all our books, all our magazines. I am quite involved in the creative process of all we do. I think I'm a good, creative partner, but I think that the creative people run into the real depth of my passion and of my energy, and I think that they probably feel overwhelmed by it at times.

But none of us has very long on this Earth to use whatever our gifts are, and I have a huge sense of urgency about getting this job done. I need all the good help I can get and the good helpers love to be part of it.

Q: What will it be to get it done in your view? When will you be finished?

A: I don't know.

Q: How big do you want the company to be? Is there an optimal size?

A: You know, we have never set an ultimate financial goal to grow the company to a certain size. This is another rule we break. We set in place what we want to get done. Then we do very strict operating plans, budgets, and performance assessments. This is a very disciplined business process. Each of the operating divisions says this is what we can do, this is where we're going, this is the revenue we can drive given the product we want to introduce, and this is the profit we can drive. And the end result of this process is our top line and bottom line goal for the year.

It never dawns on me that I should squeeze people for the next tenth of a percent of profit or the next million dollars of growth. These people are as excited as I am to drive this company to make our mark as big as we can make it. But we drive hard because we want to have more of an impact on girls. So I've never said we have to have a 10% growth or a 20% growth. Fortunately we've been well above that for ten years. But we don't come from the place of driving the business by arbitrary financial goals.

Q: So there's no plan to make Pleasant Company public in the near future?

A: No. Now why would I want to do that? There are a lot of people to answer to when you go public. We want to answer to our customers. And I suppose I answer to my own desires of what I think would make this a better company. I'm the primary stockholder. I don't need the money. We're here for girls. That's who I want to worry about, not stockbrokers.

Q: Talk a little about Addy, the American Girl doll who began life in slavery.

A: She's a black girl of the Civil War who starts her life in our first book in slavery. It's the story of her mother and her escape with her mother to the North and their early days in the free North. Because I am white and most of this company is white, we wanted to make sure that we really were doing what black parents, black educators, and black historians felt should be done for their daughters. So our first step was to establish a black Advisory Board.

Their unanimous insistence was that we tell what they considered to be the universal story of American blacks, which is that their roots are in slavery in this country. They felt this was a very important story for us to tell. They guided us through this. Addy's stories are wonderful moving stories about a girl and her mother and their struggles to be free. Of all that I have done at Pleasant Company, the one thing I think I am the proudest of is that through Addy we made a black doll an object of status and desire for white girls. Not just black girls, but white girls, too.

So many people, black or white, have said, 'We didn't ever tell our child the story of slavery.' Many parents who have said you have given us entree to discuss a difficult subject. Many girls have written us and said they had no idea what being a slave meant. It appalls me that our schools don't teach this. But the truth of it is, they don't, and I think we did a good job with this difficult subject.

Q: What do you think is the most fun thing that you do on a given day?

A: I think it's the huge variety of what I do. I have a short attention span. And this business is so multifaceted, and it plays to so many of my interests and strengths as an individual, that the variety of it is very stimulating. The creative people that surround me stimulate me, the business challenges stimulate me. I love what I learn. I like the crises as much as I like the easy days. I love the hours I spend in product development and I still spend them there after ten years. I love the times spent reading manuscripts. I love the times dreaming up a whole new idea and putting a whole new aspect of this enterprise in place. I have a very, very rich work life here.

Q: You read every manuscript of every book?

A: Yes.

Q: That's a lot of books.

A: But this is what we're about. And they're good. And I want to make sure they are.

Q: When you began Pleasant Company you were up against companies with millions of dollars in advertising budgets, promotion budgets. How did you cut through the din that's out there, competing for attention among the American public? How did you, a small company with very little financial sources, do that?

A: Well, I think we found the appropriate marketing medium in direct mail. It's a very effective targeted way of communicating to people. And it was a nascent industry or certainly a young industry at the time. And I think this company would have failed if we had gone to Toys 'R' Us and tried to get shelf space in the doll department.

We had a relatively complex story to tell. It had nuances and subtleties that related to issues like values and moral perspective that don't sell very well in the neon environment of the toy store today.

So I really think it was a great match of medium to message. Then I just cannot tell you how hungry America is for something different. The me-too-ism in the marketing departments of the world is what America is tired of. I'm tired of it when I watch my television set, I'm tired of it when I flip through magazines, I'm tired of it on billboards. I really think that slick, sound bites of sixty-second commercials have become the white noise of American life today.

People are hungry for depth and for meaning and for thoughtful, subtle ideas. We put that forth to them in our product lines and catalogs. And we are really talking *to* their kids, not at them. We are talking to their kids like they are intelligent beings. Not stupid, mindless little people. We ourselves had been intelligent little girls when we were growing up, and we had smart daughters and nieces, and we knew how we talked to them. Why can't the other products out there talk to kids that way? We are coming from a perspective that must be very foreign because we're a lonely voice.

I've never worked at a big corporation. I have no idea what the thought process is, as they develop a product, but at Pleasant Company we come from a point of sincerity, of wanting to change lives, not from a point of wanting to sell a whole lot of product.

That's how we got the market, even though that wasn't really our intention. Our intention was to be an alternative. But the market came to us, because it's starving for what we offer— quality, values, excellence. It's not that hard. What we did is not that complex. We just didn't follow the leader.

Q: Now you're the leader, and people are following you. Are you going to change your way of business with the increased competition that you're attracting?

A: I think the principles that we founded this company on and that we live by today are pretty timeless. And I think there will always be intelligent, thoughtful people wanting good quality things for their daughters. I think we'll stay the course and try to give people what we think is good for little girls and what little girls tell us they want in a way that treats them as thoughtful, intelligent beings. That's pretty unusual in the world of marketing to kids.

I don't think we're going to go on Saturday morning TV with fifteen-second commercials. I can't tell our story in fifteen seconds. This is something very, very different. Pleasant Company is about making a difference in girls' lives. It doesn't happen in sound bites, and it doesn't happen overnight. It's been an eleven-year journey to this moment of being recognized as an industry leader or pioneer. It's one foot ahead of the next, day after day after day. And we've been very blessed. We haven't made a lot of mistakes yet. Could we? Yes. Sure. But we try to do it as smart and sincerely as we can. And we don't look over our shoulder.

We are not the first doll company. There have always been dolls out there for girls. We are not the first publishing company that publishes for children or girls. There are lots of children's book publishers. We're not the first people to publish historical fiction for girls. There is lots of historical fiction out there. We are not the only catalog company that sells children's products. We are unique for one thing. We have targeted little girls as intelligent, important people, and we talk to them that way. And their parents appreciate that. And that's what matters here. And that's why we're successful.

I do think that we could make some mistakes today and probably survive it. The scary thing about being an entrepreneur is that in those early years you have no idea which piece could put you under if you don't do it right. And so you become hypervigilant. I think that's what makes entrepreneurs very difficult to work for, because even in your own heart you're not sure what piece you can blow.

And therein lies the exhaustion and the stress of building an idea from nothing—every single thread in that tapestry has to be solid and firm and tight and good. And it doesn't happen slapdash. You put a lot of energy into each thread you weave. That's really what we have done. We don't bring out a whole lot of products, we don't try to do more than we can do well, and we put those pieces in place very carefully and very thoughtfully. When we take our eyes off the ball, it gets shoddy, we know it, and we at least know to pull back and go back at it again until we get it right. That's what makes me hard to work for, because I know there's right, and I know there's the best, and we will keep going for that. If there are people out there that can run this race with us, God love them. But they're going to have to run awful fast.

Q: How would you like to be remembered?

A: Allow me, if you will, a favorite quote from Yeats: 'Look up in the sun's eye and see what the exultant heart calls good, that some new day may breed the best because we gave, not what they would, but the right twigs for an eagle's nest.'

I think we built a good eagle's nest.

CHAPTER FIVE

PAUL VOLCKER

FORMER CHAIRMAN,
FEDERAL RESERVE
BOARD

> > >

PAUL VOLCKER

FORMER CHAIRMAN, FEDERAL RESERVE BOARD

The first thing you notice about Paul Volcker is this: He is a giant. He stands approximately 6 feet 8 inches tall. But his demeanor does not intimidate. He is soft-spoken. This is a man who knows he doesn't have to shout.

Paul Volcker has a reputation among the political press, the folks who stalked him when he was Federal Reserve Board chairman, of being controlled, laconic, monosyllabic, terse. He is the opposite. Here, he is expansive, warm, and witty.

The job of Federal Reserve chairman is a balancing act: One of keeping the economy stable and growing simultaneously. Put very simply, the Fed chairman does this by either restricting the amount of money available to the banking system or by loosening it.

Think supply and demand. As is the case with any commodity, when there's too much available, the value of the item decreases. If the world were awash in Beluga caviar, for instance, it would no longer command the premium price of $3 a gram.

So it is with money. If there's too much floating around, its value is cheapened—and that means consumers need more money to buy goods. Such a scenario is also commonly known as *inflation.*

If there's too little money around, its value becomes greater. This presents problems because industry needs money for growth. When money is restricted, companies can't invest in equipment, training, or other necessary resources, for instance. Bad for business, bad for the financial markets.

Such are the worries, vastly simplified, of the Federal Reserve chairman. Add to those worries the political pressures that are always exerted on the man who holds the money lever and you have a potential for an exasperating and troubling job. It was Paul Volcker's fast grip on the money lever back in the inflation-ravaged early 1980s that made him famous. Volcker was the man who broke the back of the inflation that had dogged and decimated the American economy since 1975. And, by killing off that crippling inflation, Volcker laid the foundation for the biggest bull market in American history. In 1982, the Dow Jones industrial average stood at 821. Fifteen years later, it's neared 8,000.

Volcker laughs off the idea that he is the father of the massive move in equities that has created so much wealth in this nation. He's far too modest and far too conservative to believe such a thing. But it is true, in this way: Had he not reduced inflation in the United States, the stock market would not have performed as astoundingly as it subsequently did. Plain and simple.

One of the biggest challenges Volcker faced as chairman of the Federal Reserve was maintaining his distance from the presidents who appointed him—in this case, Jimmy Carter and Ronald Reagan—and the political situations they created. "The Federal Reserve system was set up to provide a separation from what we like to call passing political pressures or partisan politics," says Volcker. "It was set up quite independently. Now does that lead to strange conflicts? Sometimes it does. But fooling around with money for political purposes can be very dangerous. It would not be a good thing for the country or for the stability of its money."

As Volcker points out, when confidence in the stability of the American dollar is lost, both the stock market and the bond market go south. The result? A potential for crisis. "So the sense is to remove [the Fed] from the immediate den of politics, make it as professional an institution as you can. It must have a sense of integrity and continuity," he says.

Integrity, professionalism, continuity. All are traits that Volcker inherited from his parents. His mother, Alma Louise— valedictorian of her class at Vassar—got married right out of college and had five children. His father, for whom Volcker was named, was a city manager in Teaneck, New Jersey, who wound up cleaning up a corrupt town on the verge of economic ruin.

Paul Volcker was born September 5, 1927, in Cape May, New Jersey. "I grew up in an atmosphere where my father was a very prominent official in the town. I was always conscious of the fact that among other things I shouldn't do anything to embarrass him," says Volcker.

"He was a very disciplined person who wanted to make sure the town operated in a way that was beyond any question," Volcker recalls. "I remember he created a bit of a disturbance when he insisted that police and other employees didn't accept any tips at Christmastime. It was not a welcome idea but it was characteristic of his view that a public official was supposed to be beyond any question in terms of his motivations." Volcker's father saved the town from bankruptcy.

The son was graduated from Princeton University summa cum laude in 1949, he received his Masters at Harvard University in 1951. The following year, he began work as an economist at the Federal Reserve Bank of New York where he remained until 1957. With the exception of a stint as an economist at Chase Manhattan Bank between 1957 and 1961, Volcker remained in public service throughout most of his career. He spent nine years at the Treasury Department in Washington, then became president of the Federal Reserve Bank of New York, the largest in the 12-bank system. Then, in 1979, President Carter appointed him chairman of the Federal Reserve Board, where he remained until 1987. Now a private banker at New York City's Bankers Trust, Volcker is married and has two children. He is head of the international committee charged with recovering the millions of dollars lost by Holocaust victims in World War II and returning the funds to their rightful owners from the Swiss banks where they've been hidden for 50 years.

A public servant to the core, Volcker is troubled by what he perceives is a disregard or cynicism with which many Americans view their government. "I had a respect for public service as a respectable profession," he says. "We've tended to lose a lot of that in this country. There's a lack of faith in government, some of which is justified. It's a serious matter. A certain degree of skepticism should be a part of our culture, but when it turns into an eroding cynicism, I think we're in trouble."

Volcker agrees, though, that during the 1960s and 1970s, Americans came to expect that their government could solve problems of all kinds—even social problems, previously the realm of the family. "I think you can make a good argument that government tried to do too much," he says. "And in trying to do some things that it wasn't particularly well-suited for, has brought a certain amount of skepticism about the whole process. So maybe some retreat is not that unreasonable."

Perhaps even more dangerous than cynicism, though, is the complacency that Volcker believes has crept into our lives, particularly the view that inflation is gone forever.

"Inflation is never dead and buried," he says. "Unfortunately, there's always the temptation to try to speed up the economy by creating more money and taking some risk in inflation. Once you begin thinking that way, inflation has a way of creeping up on you."

This extraordinary economist also has insights into the current euphoria found in the stock market and the increasingly powerful private pools of capital that roil the international currency, stock, and bond markets. He has ideas to solve the coming Social Security crisis.

A conversation with Paul Volcker, the most famous of the 14 Federal Reserve chairmen in American history, is a rare encounter with a brilliant mind.

➤ ➤ ➤

Q: You were the chairman of the Federal Reserve Board from 1977 to 1985. Could we start with some basics about what the Federal Reserve Board is and what it does? What are the duties of the chairman and the members of the Fed?

A: Well, the Federal Reserve is America's central bank. Central banks are responsible for issuing the money that you have in your pocket. But, the economically significant thing is that they have instruments for controlling the total supply of money across the country which includes not only the currency in your pocket, but the entire volume of bank deposits. They may do this by various indirect means, but by controlling the money supply the Fed also influences interest rates and controls economic activity. It can influence the rate of inflation in the country, as well. Central banks these days are more and more dedicated to the fundamental proposition that their primary role is to stabilize the price level of the country's currency.

Q: So the role of the Federal Reserve Chairman then is to keep the economy stable. Would that be a good layman's definition?

A: Yes, stable and growing. You want economic growth over a period of time as well as stability. But, I think most central banks these days start from the proposition that to have a growing economy, you also want a stable economy, meaning reasonable price stability. Now, central banks typically have other responsibilities as well, particularly supervision and oversight of the financial system. In general, regulating and supervising the banking system; that's true in the United States. Other agencies also have a role. The Federal Reserve as the central bank has the central role.

Q: When was the Federal Reserve started?

A: The law was passed in 1913. I think it actually started in 1914.

Q: Why was it not created before that?

A: That's a good question. Central banks can be controversial institutions. There was something like a central bank in the first bank of the United States back in the end of the 18th century, shortly after the country started. It became politically controversial. There was a second bank of the United States that President Andrew Jackson was not particularly enamored of. And then the banking system went off in different directions for almost a century.

The system was relatively unregulated except in the sense that the United States was basically on the gold standard during most of that period. So, the supply of money was basically regulated by the need to maintain a stable gold price.

Q: Meaning that the value of the currency was tied to the price of gold?

A: That's right. It would go up and down, but there wasn't any long-term inflationary trend. And it was basically tied to gold. There was controversy as to whether it should be tied to gold or silver and there were a lot of arcane arguments. But most of the world was on the gold standard at that time.

Q: So, given that the United States had lived for quite a few years without a Federal Reserve or a central bank, why was it then created in 1913?

A: Because there had been repeated banking panics and crises. There was a particularly severe banking crisis in 1907, but there'd been a big depression in the 1890s and recurrent panics before that. The United States was relatively late in creating a central bank because there was some fear of undue centralization of authority.

Q: You mentioned earlier that President Jackson did not like the concept of a central bank. This brings up the question of political pressures that are exerted on the Federal Reserve. Could you describe the history of the political pressures on the central bank and what it means?

A: The Federal Reserve is a very complicated institution the way it is set up, because it was begun as a compromise between those who wanted some control and those who wanted to have an institution strong enough and flexible enough to prevent financial panics. But, there was this fear of Wall Street control.

So, it was set up with 12 different Federal Reserve banks around the country which share the authority for the decision making. And those 12 Federal Reserve banks still exist, they still have an influence on policy. The idea that you could have a different monetary policy in San Francisco than in New York or in Atlanta, which was an illusion some people had, has long since disappeared. But, you do have this regional ingredient in the system.

The board in Washington has a chairman with overall authority over the system. But the presidents of the various Federal Reserve banks participate in decision making in the administration.

Now this setup has two purposes. You get regional input. It's not an inside-the-Beltway institution by any means. At the same time, it's meant to provide an independence from what we like to call passing political pressures or partisan political pressures. And it does. The Board members serve terms of 14 years. The chairman, who has to be a member with a term of 14 years, if he serves that long, has a term of four years. These people can't be removed except for real dereliction of duty or loss of sanity or whatever. So, it was deliberately set up quite independently.

It is considered an instrument of Congress. The Congress was given the authority to print and control the value of money by the Constitution. So, a derivative from that congressional provision was the congressional authority to set up the Federal Reserve which then reports to Congress. The Fed must testify before Congress. It's accountable to the Congress; it is not directly accountable to the president. The president appoints the members of the Board, but the president cannot order the Federal Reserve to take action.

Now, does that lead to strange conflicts? Sometimes it does. The independence of the Federal Reserve and the independence of other central banks is to prevent the temptation to fool around with money for political purposes, which can be very dangerous. And if people try to use monetary policy for electoral purposes, it would not be a good thing for the country; it would not be a good thing for the stability of money.

And if you lose confidence in the stability of money, you have a very bad environment for the bond market, for the stock market.

Q: And a potential for a crisis.

A: And a potential for a crisis. So, the sense was to remove the Fed from the immediate den of politics, make it as professional an institution as you can. I think it's terribly important that it has a sense of integrity and continuity. And provide an institution that can maintain credibility and confidence. And that is the effort. And I think we've been pretty successful through the years in the United States, and in other countries too.

Q: Now, what is the role of the chairman?

A: To preside. Seriously, the chairman of the board is basically the public spokesman for the system, and he is the one to deal primarily with other central banks, to report to the Congress directly. Obviously there's got to be a lot of relationships with the Secretary of the Treasury, with the president, with the administration. And he is the one who basically conducts that. He has only one vote, like other members of the board, and the so-called committee which controls monetary policy. Technically the chairman has only one vote, but he is the one in the public eye and is looked to for direction, perhaps more than is appropriate. Now, we've got the so-called Greenspan policy. Well, Alan Greenspan is one of the 12 members of the open market committee, and one of the 7 members of the board. But, there's no doubt that you look to the chairman for leadership.

Q: And the chairman is the one who also gets the political pressure?

A: There's no question about that.

Q: Let's talk a little bit about your background. You've been a public servant for a great part of your career. Your father was also a public servant.

A: That's right; I suppose I inherited that.

Q: Tell us about him and what his impact on your life was.

A: Well, my father was one of the first city managers. That is a profession that really only started during his early lifetime. And I grew up in an atmosphere where he was a very prominent official in my hometown.

Q: That was Teaneck, New Jersey?

A: Yes, and it was growing rapidly at that time. He was a city manager elsewhere, too. But when I was in my formative years he was in Teaneck.

Q: Wasn't Teaneck at that time reputed to have corruption through and through?

A: Well, that's an exaggeration. But, it was on the verge of bankruptcy when he took over right at the beginning of the Depression. And it was kind of an old boy's circle in some ways in its management, and he professionalized the administration, there ain't any question about that. Rescued it, first of all, from bankruptcy. But, it became quite well known as kind of a model town. It was picked out after the war, they did an early television show about city management—and sent it over to Europe—about how an American town was managed. He was pretty well known.

Q: What was his secret? What did he do that was so crucial?

A: I don't think it was any one thing, but he was a pretty disciplined person who was sure that the town was going to operate in a way that was beyond any question. I remember when I got older he created a bit of a disturbance when he insisted that the town police and other city employees didn't accept any tips at

Christmastime. He tried to enforce that which was not exactly welcome. But, it was characteristic of his view that a public official was supposed to be beyond question in terms of his motivations. He used to make an annual budget for the town and describe all his policies and what they were about—very detailed: How many new policemen were being hired or fired or whatever—and distributed it to everybody in the town, which was rather unusual.

Q: That kind of openness is unusual.

A: Yes. And growing up, I was always conscious of the fact that among other things I shouldn't do anything to embarrass him. I was conscious of that position. In my eyes anyway he was the most prominent citizen in the town. And that probably affected me indirectly and directly in many ways. But, I had a kind of respect for public service as a respectable profession. And, I think, we have tended to lose a lot of that in this country. I think it's a serious problem. There's cynicism about government—a certain degree of skepticism should be part of our culture—but when it turns into an eroding cynicism, I think we're in trouble.

And it's going in that direction and I feel it myself. So, coming from a background of my father being a public official, until he retired and did a little teaching, this lack of faith in government, some of which is justified, is a serious matter.

Q: Do you think there's a solution?

A: Well, I think it's a hard struggle. We've got to improve our processes of government in a lot of different directions. I think different things require different attention. Campaign finance reform is very much on everybody's mind. Money has always been very much there in politics, but it's become even more overpowering in recent years.

Then again, I think you can make a good argument that government has tried to do too much in recent years. And in trying to do some things that it wasn't particularly well suited for has brought a certain amount of skepticism about the whole process. So, maybe some retreat is not that unreasonable.

Q: Tell me about your mother. What was she like?

A: Well, my mother came from upstate New York and went to Vassar College. Graduated first in her class, and then became a housewife. But, you know, it was an interesting age. This woman who was obviously very talented and today would go off and do something exotic, essentially married my father and brought up five children.

Q: Well, that's a big job.

A: Yeah it was. And she was active in local community affairs and church affairs. She died only a few years ago at the age of 98.

Q: You've got some good genes. So, you grew up in a family of five children?

A: Well, I really grew up with four. One of them died quite young. But, I had three older sisters that I grew up with. I was the baby.

Q: And you went to Princeton for your undergraduate degree, and Harvard for graduate school?

A: I went to Harvard, and I spent a year at the London School of Economics. And then actually went into the Federal Reserve as an economist where I worked for some summers. I'd been in and out of the Federal Reserve, the Treasury Department, and the Chase Manhattan Bank for awhile. I became president of the New York Federal Reserve Bank, which is the biggest, most operational of those 12 Federal Reserve banks.

In 1979 when the economy was not doing very well, when inflation was accelerating, I became Chairman of the Board.

Q: On the subject of inflation: You are perhaps best known for breaking the back of the crippling inflation that hit the United States in the late '70s, early '80s after the oil crisis. How did you do it?

A: How did I do it? We had a lot tighter reign on money than we had had before. That's the tool the Federal Reserve has in its armory. We restricted the growth in the money supply. And you had a lot of inflationary momentum; to sustain high inflation you need more money in the system. You can't keep an inflationary process going without people having more money that they can spend to maintain the higher prices on goods.

Q: Inflation is more money chasing fewer goods.

A: At the end of the process, and with a lot of complications but, yes, inflation is fed by an increase in the money supply. Too much money chasing too few goods, as you say. And we restricted the supply of money. There's nothing, in any sense, new about that except we did it in a more disciplined way and in a more public way really. We kind of staked our flag to the mast saying we were going to restrict the money supply in a way that could be clearly observed.

It was a very tough period because the demand for money was very high. People didn't believe that inflation could be made to disappear. They'd gotten used to inflation, they were anticipating inflation. And so you had a big demand for money. You didn't have much supply. And interest rates got much higher than any of us anticipated.

Q: Short-term interest rates went up to 21%?

A: Well, I think the prime lending rate got up to 21%, or 21.5% at one point. The Treasury bill rate didn't get that high, nor did the market rate, but, yes, the bank rates did get that high. It was a very difficult period, and we had a recession which I think was inevitable. It was a severe recession. But, the inflation rate did come down, and since then we've had much lower rates of inflation, and we've had a very good record of economic growth once we got rid of that inflation psychosis, if I can use that word. There were certainly very strong expectations for continued inflation at that time.

I suppose it's now 15, 20 years ago and maybe people are starting to forget about inflation, which is a dangerous thing. But it was the most damaging inflation we had ever had in our entire history, in its persistence. We had a bad inflation after the Civil War, we had a bad inflation for a year or two at the end of World War I, but they didn't last.

Q: And this lasted how long?

A: Well, it really began getting momentum in the early 1970s. And by 1980 it reached an annual rate of 15%. Which doesn't look so high if you're in Brazil or Argentina or other countries, but it's very high for the United States. And the screws begin coming loose in the economy in some sense when you have an inflation rate of that magnitude.

Q: Inflation basically eats away at the value of the dollar.

A: People don't want to hold money, they don't want to hold bonds.

Q: The stock market goes down.

A: It depresses the stock market because people are afraid of what the future will bring. And you had all those things going on in the early '80s. People kind of forget: The stock market in 1982 was about the same level that it was in the mid-1960s. It was a little more than 800 on the Dow Jones industrial average. We have seen enormous increases in stock values since '82 from something more than 800 to whatever it is now, more than 7,000. It's an unparalleled improvement.

Q: It's all really your doing.

A: I think the stability of expectations has had something to do with it.

Q: What was the most difficult decision you had to make as Fed chairman? Was it during that time?

A: Well, you can say it was difficult. But, it was only possible because the public was ready to support a tough policy on inflation. You know, the Federal Reserve can be an independent institution by law, and it is independent. And I think it's got a good enough reputation that it's naturally got some public support. But, it can't go right against the grain of all public opinion and all political opinion. We do operate in a democracy.

But inflation had gotten bad enough so that people were scared, and they were willing to see somebody do something about it. And the Federal Reserve was the institution that is by its nature supposed to do something about it. I'm not saying we would have won a popularity contest in the country. It was a difficult, unhappy period in some respects, and there was a lot of political opposition—but we had a good deal of quiet support for what we were doing. Some of it was not so quiet. Because people did understand, I think, a very simple fact: That we were trying to do something about inflation, and that was important.

We got a lot of criticism from the White House and a lot of leaks from the Treasury. But, President Reagan never really criticized us in public because I think he had a gut instinct that we were trying to do the right thing. And he thought we should stabilize prices. And we were basically on the right track, even when it was not politically desirable at the moment. Of course, by the time the election came along in 1984 things were already on the right track and it wasn't a political problem anymore then.

Q: Inflation now, as you point out, has dropped substantially from those high levels. And there is now even talk that inflation is dead and buried.

A: It's never dead and buried. Unfortunately, there's always the temptation to try to speed up the economy by creating more money and taking some risk in inflation. And it's kind of sad for me to see a little of that opinion arising in the United States today. Not very strongly, but nonetheless can't we speed it up, just ease up money a little bit, and get the economy going a little bit faster. After all, inflation's been down, we shouldn't worry about it so much at these low levels.

Once you begin thinking in those terms which, of course, was very common in the '60s and the '70s, inflation has a way of creeping up on you. And the basic feeling is if 4% inflation is okay, well 5% can't be too bad, and if 5% isn't too bad, and you're there for awhile, let's not be too tough about preventing it from going a little higher, it can't hurt us. And that's very insidious because it begins building on itself—and then you're in trouble.

But it's interesting that in the past 15 years in many countries around the world, there's almost been a sort of new religion about the importance of price stability. There has been a very clear movement toward making central banks around the world independent, if they weren't independent; more independent if they were independent. The Federal Reserve hasn't changed, but we were among the most independent to start with. The Bundesbank in Germany, which was actually modelled on the Federal Reserve, has always been very independent. The new currency discussion in Europe says as part of the rules every central bank in Europe has to have a statute assuring its own independence for the European system to work.

In Latin America, central banks have become independent. There's talk in Japan now about making the Bank of Japan more formally independent. And it's just true all over the world, recognizing, I think, the importance of a strong central bank and the importance of stability.

Q: Some of the current discussion on the death of inflation centers on the idea that because we're now in a world economy where money will seek the highest rates of return wherever they are, that labor costs will continue to drop because new countries will have lower labor costs and that that will continue to keep inflation low. Do you agree?

A: Well, I think the world economy has had a restraining influence on prices in the particular period we're in. But I don't think globalization is quite as new as some of the talk. There's no question that the cheapness of communication and transportation, plus the opening of markets, has made the world even more competitive than it was. And you have countries— take the extreme example, China, with a billion and a quarter people coming on the world market—with very low labor costs. This has an impact.

But, I think we should not forget that this period of intense international competition and free availability of goods is taking place in a time when Europe has not been growing, Japan has not been growing. They both have exceptionally high levels of unemployment. Japan not so high statistically, but high in their own context. Europe is running unemployment rates of more than 10%.

You look at those situations, if they got a little growth momentum back, this easy availability and strong competition in world markets may look a little different. And if you have a kind of synchronized expansion in the world economy, which from one point of view you want to have, you're not going to have the same benign environment in terms of inflation. So, we have to be on guard.

Q: In your book *Changing Fortunes,* you talk of various economic summits and economic agreements that have been struck between the various nations, economic powers over the years. And you discuss the problem of governments meddling with their currencies, which the Economic Summit of 1975 was supposed to stop. Isn't this always a threat? Isn't it really a pipe dream that governments are not going to try to meddle in currencies?

A: Well, they will sometimes try to meddle for different purposes. The Europeans worry about that more than Americans do because of the close competition between European nations. And the integration of those economies makes it particularly difficult to have currency instability. One country may try to make their currency cheap to assist their industry, because their goods will be cheaper elsewhere. But it won't work long term.

There's been some brouhaha in Europe in recent years, particularly about Italy depreciating too much. And that's part of the force behind the idea of having a single currency in Europe, to avoid that. But, my concern more recently has been simply the fact that there is too much instability and too much volatility, whether or not people deliberately try to manipulate their currencies. It's not so much a question of deliberate manipulation in my view at this point, but the instabilities associated with a failure to demonstrate the necessary leadership among governments to determine which exchange rates are reasonably natural and competitive and to defend them, so that you don't have these very wide swings. People like to think they will go away at some point, but they don't seem to go away because we recently had a swing of almost 40% again with the Japanese yen.

The yen was at 80 to a dollar not so long ago. Now it's 112, whatever it is. That's a big swing percentage-wise, and people begin worrying oh, isn't it unfair, too many Toyotas can be sold in the United States at too-cheap prices. Things were just getting competitive. Where do you know how to invest when currencies swing to that degree? Frankly, I think that is a real problem that economists underestimate. And governments really don't want to deal with it, because, understandably, they don't want to undertake commitments that they can't enforce and meet.

And they're afraid that they may run into conflicts between stabilizing currency exchange rate values in ways that will undermine domestic policy. I think that fear is overblown, but it exists.

Q: The conflict behind the single currency for Europe seems almost to be the whole idea of meddling with the currency, that is, setting it at a certain rate.

A: It depends what you call meddling. I don't think it's meddling exactly. It would, in fact, create one currency for Europe that you can't meddle with. It's fixed. There's nothing you can do about it, which is the object.

Now there are two dimensions to that. One is there won't be any exchange rate changes within Europe. You can't meddle by definition. And second, then the question is what happens to that single currency? Will it be stable or not?

There's been a tremendous focus on what these central banks can do to make sure that the new currency is stable. And that's a large part of what all the fight is about. The Germans say look, we have a strong, stable currency. And we're not going to give up our beloved Deutsch mark to something that's going to be called the Euro. But, we want to make sure the Euro is as stable as the Yen is. And we want institutions that will assure that. And they have a very strong statute in the treaty assuring the independence of the European central bank. It goes beyond anything—so far as I know—that any national government has because they want to lean over backwards to ensure the authority in the central bank. Ensure not only its authority but also the stability of the currency.

Q: So, you think this can work, and you think it will reduce the volatility?

A: Well, it will certainly reduce currency volatility within Europe, because you're going to have to eliminate the different currencies within Europe. You won't see the fluctuations in the national currency because they don't exist anymore. You can debate whether it will increase the stability between European currencies and the dollar and the yen, and that's where I would say the three areas ought to get together. What I suggested: Don't you think of some rate that looks reasonably competitive, and let things fluctuate plus or minus 10%, which is at the extremes 20%, but at least commit yourself to maintaining that kind of range which is much narrower than what's been happening frequently in the market in recent years.

And that would give a better base for business planning, a better base for continuing reasonable competition, a better base for maintaining open markets in other directions, avoiding excessive protectionist pressures.

I haven't sold that story yet.

Q: One of the developments in recent years that's a little alarming is the size of the private pools of capital that are always seeking investment value and high returns wherever they can get them around the world. Some of these pools are larger than or can overwhelm central banks. They're unregulated, unlike the banks in this country. What's your view on this?

A: Well, I would argue that's why governments and central banks ought to take a stronger position on currency values. The popular fear, and the fear in some central banks, is they'd be overwhelmed by these speculators or investors. And they will be overwhelmed if their basic policies are not consistent and in accordance with stability. You can't defend against those kinds of private funds and trillions of dollars if you are conducting policies that are unrealistic and are bound to create tensions and changes in currency values. So, there's a certain discipline required.

But, if you can maintain a discipline of general stability and confidence, then I think those market forces will tend to work with you rather than against you. Now, the market has no very clear idea as to which currency values are appropriate. And so their expectations swing anywhere in the world. Not so much within Europe, where they've been defending them, but outside of Europe. So, the values of the currencies swing widely because they really don't know where they should be. That's part of the problem.

Another part of the problem which overlaps, but it is different, is if you're a smaller country—not the United States, not Europe, not Japan—you can be overwhelmed by what appear to be fairly marginal shifts of funds by institutions, by mutual funds, by speculators. They can move 3% of their money, but 3% of their money may be equal to your whole money supply. And that's a special kind of problem, which I don't think anybody has a very good solution for.

But, the domestic markets can get swamped by this international availability of money. And you like to think of the market as all-seeing and all-knowing and making very orderly adjustments, but clearly it does not. Mexico is the prime example. Money poured in there for three or four years. But then something happened—partly politically, partly otherwise—to indicate that too much money was going in there, and so it was withdrawn. And you have a tremendous crisis. It wasn't an orderly adjustment.

Q: So can these private investors or mutual funds or whatever have a good influence as well? In that they will keep central bankers honest?

A: I think they can have a good influence, particularly in the bigger countries. But, I think the leading countries have really failed in developing better leadership as to what appropriate exchange rates are and how to defend them. And those flows should be more benign in an atmosphere in which the rules were a little clearer, let me put it that way.

Q: As far as the competitiveness of America, do you feel on the global stage that America is as competitive as she needs to be?

A: Well, certainly. But, we still have big deficits in current account and trade account. We run a surplus in services, overall we have a big deficit which can't be sustained forever, and it's really inappropriate for the biggest, wealthiest country in the world and a world leader to be running these perpetual deficits. How does that reconcile with the fact that these days, unlike ten years ago, you have a sense that American industry feels pretty competitive. And by a lot of measures, in world markets, things produced in the United States are cheap, sophisticated products. And we're the clear leaders in technology and modern electronics. So, what's going on here? Why don't we see it in the trade balance?

I think part of that is what I mentioned earlier about the sluggishness of the economy in Europe and Japan. While we've been growing at sustainable speed, they haven't been growing. Not growing, or growing almost imperceptibly. They've got a lot of excess capacity. If they began growing faster, I think you would find our innate competitiveness showing in the figures a little better. And the other thing is, of course, in many areas some of those eastern Asian countries in particular are highly competitive, and we and other countries do a lot of importing from them.

Q: But overall you're optimistic?

A: Well, overall, I think the American industry is in pretty good shape internationally. Of course there's been a big decline in the dollar, too, which over the years has made us more competitive.

Q: Let's talk a little bit about China, which as you mentioned earlier is an enormous potential market for a lot of American companies. Given its size, and other countries like India that are just coming out of the Dark Ages, do you believe there's enough capital in the world, cheap enough capital to bring those countries up to modern age?

A: Well, in general, my answer would be yes. As much capital as you would like to see, my answer would be no. These countries—Asia in particular, and I would think this pattern would certainly be followed in China—are capable, in the early stages of development, of generating a big amount of capital themselves, which is where most of them come from. Their savings rates are enormous.

Americans save net 3 to 4% of gross domestic product. And that's the biggest single source of capital. The foreign capital can provide a useful margin, and it should. But, if you ask me whether the United States is generating as much savings as it should for its own welfare, much less China's or India's, the answer is clearly no. We are, pitifully, at the bottom of the international league. We worry how we're going to support an aging population with a declining savings rate—a problem. And we're surviving so far by borrowing a lot from abroad.

You've got this rather ironic situation where again the world leader is the world's biggest debtor. And you wonder whether this can go on forever, and I think it can't.

Q: What can we do about the low savings rate in America?

A: Well, Americans like to spend, there's no question about that. And I don't know what it takes to change a very basic ingrained behavior pattern in the United States. But, you're not going to do it by tinkering around the edges, in my opinion.

The first and most obvious thing you do is balance the federal budget. That's a form of dis-saving, a form of borrowing. Ideally we should be running a surplus in the budget. So that is number one.

Q: Do you think that can be achieved with the balanced budget amendment?

A: Well, I have not been thrilled with the balanced budget amendment. I'd certainly like to see a balanced budget. And I'd like to see a surplus. I don't know whether I want all the rigidities and legal problems that a balanced budget amendment would bring. I've almost come to the point where maybe it is a good idea. But we are making some progress on the budget. We're not making it as fast as we should. But, that's number one.

187

Number two, if you want to change it through other government policies, I think you've got to think about a really radical change in the tax system, which of course gets debated now and then. I don't know what the prospects are, but our tax system is hard on savings.

Q: It actually punishes savings.

A: Yes. And we've got to move toward a tax system that favors savings. We try to do it by fooling around the edges, with 401(k) plans and IRAs and that sort of thing. And I think the results of that looks good individually, but if you look at the total amount of savings in the country, it has continued to be very weak. So, it takes stronger medicine. I think it takes a heavier emphasis on consumption taxes, and away from taxes on investment. And it's as simple as that. And it's as simple as that for me to say; it's not very easy to do.

Q: Would that include taking away the double taxation on dividends, on interest?

A: That's part of it. Most countries in the world have the value added tax, which is a tax on consumption, where a substantial part of tax revenues come directly from taxing sales. There are proposals for something resembling the present income tax where you exempt all savings.

That's almost a reverse of what we do now. And I think in terms of encouraging savings, encouraging productivity, encouraging growth it would be a good idea. But, it's a big challenge to move from what we've got now in a fair way to something like that.

Q: Balancing the budget is a goal that many have tried unsuccessfully to achieve. We are making some progress on it. Is the deficit still a concern to you?

A: Yes, because the deficit decreases savings. The lower the savings, the lower the investment you have, the more costly your investment will be; the lower the investment you have, the lower the growth; the lower the productivity of the economy, the lower the growth of the economy. It's as simple as that. If you want to have 2.5% growth, you want to move to 3.5% growth, you need more investment. You can't get more investment without more savings. And after awhile that 1% difference adds up to 50% of gross domestic product in the next generation, when many people are going to be retired and you're going to have to rely upon all that increased productivity.

Q: One of the balances that the Federal Reserve has to strike is between regulation and allowing the free markets to operate in the best possible way. How does the Fed strike that balance?

A: This is an important issue that Congress has not been willing to address in recent years. Things have been changing rapidly in the financial world—technology and institutions can do with great ease things that they couldn't do some years ago, whether in the United States or internationally. The money market fund depends upon a technology that didn't exist before. Banks used to have a monopoly on lending, because they had certain skills. No longer.

Used to be, if you had money to invest or money you wanted to maintain for spending, you had to go to a bank. Now you have a lot of different institutions you can go to. Money market funds, mutual funds, hedge funds. But Federal Reserve regulation, financial regulation in most countries, is based upon regulating banks. Well, banks aren't as important as they used to be.

Securities firms are now as big as banks. That creates competitive problems. You don't want to put banks at a disadvantage. But, if you think there has to be some regulation and supervision in the financial system, what do you do? Do you extend your regulation to those new institutions? Do you relax the regulation on the banks? You do some of both.

It's very discouraging to me to see the inability of the Congress for 15 years to effectively legislate, to give the Federal Reserve and the other authorities what seem to me a reasonable authority and flexibility for dealing with this situation. It's inherently difficult to deal with anyway. But, the market has been growing up around the old hierarchy and old establishments. Yet it's hard to reach a political consensus on sensible legislation.

Meanwhile, the regulators reinterpret existing law in ways that, to an old conservative like me, seem very strange. But, they do it because of the inability of the Congress to act. It involves much more cooperation between national authorities, which is very complicated, which has been achieved to a remarkable extent in banking. There are essentially common capital requirements for banks all around the world now. They never existed before, which is a kind of key element in banking supervision.

Q: It's almost as though a crisis will have to occur for anything to get done.

A: A common affliction of democracy I'm afraid. Much too often you don't act except in the face of crisis.

The big area where a lot of people worry with some justice is what we do with the so-called entitlement programs. They're going to take more and more of our money. The population is aging rapidly, particularly in a decade or two. You should begin preparing for that now. But, it's very hard to get political change, as you know, for something that's going to happen with some certainty 15 or 20 years from now.

Q: What would be your best idea for how to solve the coming Social Security bankruptcy?

A: One obvious thing is to increase the Social Security retirement age. Retirement age was set at 65, when that was an average age expectancy. Now the average life expectancy is some eight or nine years higher. Many people are working, and able to work, and want to work beyond 65. There has been legislation to raise the retirement age very gradually, but it ought to be speeded up, and that saves you a lot of money over time.

Maybe you can face up to some increase in payroll tax, but the payroll tax is already very high, and that won't take care of the whole problem, and I don't think it's right taking care of the problem that way.

The philosophical issue that will be debated, and I think has to be debated, is whether we retreat from the Social Security concept, which I personally hate to do. But, maybe we've reached the time where we can move away from the idea that everybody is entitled to a Social Security payment regardless of how relatively wealthy they are. That was kind of a principle of the first system. But, the question is whether we can still afford to pay Social Security to somebody like me who can get along without it. I hasten to say I'm not getting Social Security now, because I still work.

Q: These ideas seem to be fairly obvious and basic.

A: But they're very hard to do. The political pressures are very great. And the political pressures these days are organized, and you wonder whether the organized political pressures don't take a stronger view than the people they presumably repre-sent. And you always wonder if you took a poll of people over 65, would they be quite as hard-nosed and unyielding as the American Association of Retired People.

Once you employ somebody to represent you, they are inclined to be harder-lined than you are yourself in many cases I have found.

Q: A lot about the world has changed since 1913. How does the Fed's role differ today from when it was founded?

A: Well, I don't think the basic role differs. The instruments obviously differ some because the markets are changed. But there's surprisingly little difference in the instruments they use now compared to what they used in the 1920s. What did change certainly in the '30s was the economic philosophy in the United States and elsewhere that said the government has to take more responsibility for avoiding recessions and depressions. They should become more activist. And while the Federal Reserve was created, in effect, to avoid monetary crises and money panics, there wasn't the same feeling that the government should do something about recurrent recessions.

That became popular in the '30s during the deep Depression, the view that the government could keep the economy on an even keel, and that reached its high point in the 1960s. The Federal Reserve was part of that. And the legislation was changed and said the Federal Reserve had to worry more about growth in the economy and the speed of growth and avoiding recession. And that was part of the process by which I think we got a lot more inflation. The focus was to put more and more on growth and stability of the economy. The concern about inflation tended to get depressed a bit. And what we found out is when you forget about inflation, you get inflation and you didn't get growth and you didn't get stability in the economy either; you got just the reverse.

That was the great lesson, I think, of the 1970s and early 1980s.

Q: How do you feel about cutting taxes?

A: I think we've got to keep the deficit in mind. The tax system needs reform—I don't think there's any question about that. But, the idea of cutting taxes to spur the economy at a time when unemployment is the lowest we've had in 20 years, inflation is low, the prospects of sustainable growth are good, it's only a disturbing influence on the economic outlook in my opinion. Because reducing taxes on any broad scale, without an equivalent reduction in expenditures, is a fairy tale. Tax reduction is going to lead to bigger deficits, more expectation of inflation, and will disrupt the prospects for steady economic advance rather than improving it.

Now, the great political challenge is how we get needed reform in the tax system without trying to short-circuit the process by reducing taxes, depleting our savings at a time when we haven't got any excess savings. We haven't got the kind of savings that can . . . finance the big government deficit.

Q: One of your tasks as chairman of the Fed was to testify before Congress regularly. What was that like? These are politicians who are often trying to grandstand when they attack you. Yet you're simply trying to do your job.

A: Yes, trying to be honest and to explain clearly what's going on. I used to get accused of obfuscating, which usually, in my opinion, was not a justified complaint. Because what you try to do is explain things carefully knowing that the real world is complicated. And the political process can't stand complicated explanations. They want a clear, simple answer. Are interest rates going to go up or down? You're going to tighten the money supply or loosen? They want a clear answer. And most of the time the situation doesn't permit such clear answers on your operating techniques anyway.

The time to give a clear answer is yes, are we against inflation? Are we going to go for price stability? That should get a clear and unmuddy answer. But, when you're talking about the techniques of policy and day-to-day tactics and month-to-month tactics, it's hard to get the messages across in a clear way. But, you have a responsibility to explain yourself in a democracy. Without it, the institution isn't going to last, and your policy isn't going to be successful. And of course those opportunities to testify also give you a chance to try to, as best you can, educate the public as well as the Congress.

And so in some sense it sometimes turns into a little debate, but you can hope to turn it to your advantage. When the thing becomes purely political, you feel a little helpless and it's annoying. Once in a while you'll have a senator come in who'll read a written statement telling you that you're doing the most terrible things in the world. And before you can even respond, he basically gets up and walks out. And the television cameras are off.

Q: And someone else wrote it for him.

A: Exactly. Of course, he didn't write it for himself. And it gets a little frustrating. But, it's a part of the process. And basically it's the healthy part.

Where it would get annoying, I guess is the right word, there would be times you would go through this procedure at the beginning of a congressional session by law, where you had to report. You go before the Senate Banking Committee, the House Banking Committee, the Senate Budget Committee, the House Banking Budget Committee, an appropriation committee or two, and the Joint Economic Committee, and you do it all in the space of two weeks. You basically have the same thing to say, but each committee wants its input. And it's a little bit of overkill.

But, the process is challenging, and sometimes you *want* to testify because you've got a story to tell. And you appreciate a question that deserves an answer. If it's a purely political question, of course, it's not very enlightening and not very comfortable. But, it's a healthy part of the process.

Q: Are there any decisions that you made that you would do differently on hindsight?

A: When I look back, there is one incident that stands out as having set us back—I don't know whose mistake it was. It was an unfortunate experience, but it wasn't the end of the world. But, in the midst of the inflation, right toward the end of the Carter presidency, we had this experiment in credit controls where we directly tried to restrain borrowing. And the president himself was very enthusiastic about wanting to do this; it was going to be done, the Federal Reserve had to acquiesce.

We somewhat reluctantly acquiesced; we didn't do very much in the technical sense, but it had a very strong psychological effect. The one thing we potentially affected was the use of the growth and credit card indebtedness. And a lot of people got the idea that credit cards suddenly became unpatriotic. They weren't quite as commonly used then as now. But they were widely used. And people would send in their ripped up credit cards, and they repaid all their credit card debt, which is all fine, except consumption suddenly dropped and the economy went into recession. And it was a kind of phony recession because it was an artificial, emotional reaction to the president's call for credit controls.

A few months later we got rid of them and the economy rebounded. But, it was disturbing because people were feeling the other real recession on their hands. And I always think of it as a lost six months or lost year in terms of what we were really trying to achieve. That was the period that bothered me the most.

Nonetheless, it was a good lesson about when you think you're going to control something directly that you can have, regardless of how carefully you try to do it, very unanticipated and counterproductive results.

Q: One developing country we haven't talked about is Russia. What do you think the chances are of that country having a central bank like the Federal Reserve?

A: Well, their central bank has had growing pains, to say the least. It's had a variety of different chairmen, governors, or presidents, or whatever they call them in Russia. It has a woman chairman now. It may have been changed, but she turned out to be very tough. I think she was a woman who had come out of the central bank but she applied tougher policies than her predecessors, and they actually got the inflation rate down a lot. But, the Russian economy is very chaotic now.

And while the inflation rate has fallen remarkably from the very extreme levels they had a few years ago, there's still very little growth in the economy and a lot of disorganization. As you know, it has not been a shining example of an easy transition from a socialist state to capitalism. And I think this is a big concern, politically as well as economically.

But, in sheer inflation terms, they've done a much better job recently in supervisory terms, in terms of a stable banking system or financial system. It's a very weak financial system. It's got a very long way to go.

Q: Tell me what you do today. What's your average day like?

A: Well, I'm now a director of Bankers Trust. My average day recently has involved trying to help mediate, if that's the right word, the dispute between the Jewish community and the Swiss banking system about what happened to refugee accounts that were put in Swiss banks in the 1930s and during World War II. Obviously, it's a very emotional issue. And I am the chairman of a committee that's been established to try to work our way through that. We're still at the early stages, but we've employed some of the major accounting firms in the world to look into it, and not just in an ordinary order, but do what amounts to detective work to try to trace this as best one can after 50 or 60 years. It's not an easy task. But, controversy about it around the world has ballooned recently.

Q: And the Swiss are letting you in?

A: The Swiss are letting the accounting firms in. And will let us in terms of seeing the results, except those which can be protected. We will not see the names on particular accounts, which is the essence of the secrecy. We don't need to see that. If we find something, there can be other ways to reconcile names of the accounts with people entitled to them. But it's not going to be an easy task after 50 years. But we do intend to have an investigation that can put this question to rest. And to bring an end to this unfortunate episode in world history.

Q: What do you do in your spare time? How do you relax, if you do?

A: Well, I haven't been relaxing much recently, not as much as I should. I like to go fishing. But I do much more talking about fishing than doing it. I relax by talking about it more than going. But I do occasionally go.

Q: Where do you go?

A: Well, I go to Montana sometimes, but I've been doing some salmon fishing in recent years. Since that's a bigger proposition than going trout fishing, you tend to keep a little more on schedule. I actually went a couple of times to Russia, which opened up some salmon fishing areas. But, I try to spend a week in Iceland and go to Canada a few times a year. I try to go trout fishing once in a while, but sometimes that gets postponed. I grew up bass fishing. My father was a great bass fisherman, and we used to go out there in a row boat amid the frogs and the spinners. I spent a lot of time bass fishing in my boyhood.

Q: What do you like about it? Does it recall your boyhood for you?

A: I think that's probably part of it. You get away, and that's always something a little new and different. You go out there and see whether you can get one of these fish, which I guess are inherently pretty dumb, but seem pretty smart sometimes, to bite. It's the challenge of seeing them rise more than catching them. The fact that you put something out there and can induce them to strike at your lure.

I actually tie my own flies once in awhile. They're pretty messy, but it doesn't seem to bother the fish. Then I think, my God, I fooled them. Not only did I fool them, but I fooled them with this little piece of thread and feather and fur that I made myself.

There's a certain spirit in the chase.

HISTORICAL TIMELINES

Andrew Grove

1936   Born "Andras Grof."

1956   Left Hungarian homeland after the failed revolution.

1963   Received a PhD in chemical engineering from University of California at Berkeley. Joined Fairchild Semiconductor as an assistant to Gordon Moore.

1968   Intel became incorporated as NM Electronics (Noyce and Moore). Andrew Grove was one of only 12 initial employees.

1970   Intel produced its first successful product: the 1103 chip with 1K, a thousand bytes of dynamic random access memory (DRAM).

1971   Intel profits rose to $9.43 million due also to success of the EPROM (erasable programmable read-only memory).

1975   Grove named executive vice president as Intel prepared for expansion. As a result, Grove gained more control of production and systems management.

1978   Intel introduced new 8086/8088 chips.

1979   Intel profits surged to $661 million—gaining 40% of the microprocessor market share. Embarked on Operation Crush, a campaign to achieve 2,000 "design wins" over its competitors. Intel ended up with 2,500, including a win over IBM. Grove was named president and chief operating officer and nicknamed the "Prussian General" for his ability to lead and drive his workers.

1980   IBM chose Intel's 8088 microprocessor for its new personal computer.

1981   Grove initiated the "125 percent solution," a policy which required all professional employees to maintain 50-hour work weeks with no overtime pay.

1983   Grove published *High Output Management* in which he expounded on his theory of an "output-oriented approach to management."

1985   The price of Intel chips was driven down due to competition from companies such as Texas Instruments, Motorola, and also Japanese manufacturers.

1986   Total revenue fell from $1.6 billion in 1984 to $1.2 billion. The result was an implemented 10% pay cut, closure of eight locations, and a 30% reduction of Intel's workforce. Grove began to engineer a turnaround: Intel got out of the memory chip business and into microprocessors. Intel introduced the 386 and embarked on extensive marketing campaign to support it.

1987   Grove became chief executive officer of Intel Corporation. He published *One-On-One with Andy Grove*.

1988   Profits rose to $2.9 billion because of the successful 386. The 486 microprocessor (1% as big as the width of a human hair) was released.

1989   Developed the Pentium Processor which had 3.1 mil-
        lion transistors in a single chip. Intel scrambled to deal
        with a bug found in the Pentium. Intel also started to
        speed up the innovation timetable so that the new ver-
        sions of products replaced each other faster.

1990   An estimated 14 of the 22 million PCs in the world
        used an Intel microprocessor.

1994   Intel launched the $150 million advertising campaign,
        "Intel Inside," to market the Pentium and make Intel a
        household name.

1996   Grove was named chairman of Intel Corporation. He
        published his bestselling book, *Only the Paranoid Sur-
        vive.*

SOURCES
1. Gross, Daniel, *Forbes Greatest Business Stories of All Time*
   (New York: Wiley, 1996).
2. "Man of the Year: Intel's Andrew Grove," *Financial World*
   (December 11, 1990).

Frederick Wallace Smith

1944   Born near Memphis, Tennessee. His father, James Frederick Smith, became chairman and controlling stockholder of Dixie Greyhound Bus Lines with holdings worth $17 million upon his death in 1948.

1959   Enrolled in Memphis University School, a college preparatory school. He joined two fifteen-year-old classmates in opening "Ardent Record Company" with $5000 borrowed from their parents.

1962   Attended Yale and majored in economics and political science.

1965   At Yale, Smith wrote a term paper (not particularly well received) illustrating his innovative concept of "hub and spoke" which later determined delivery routes for Federal Express.

1966   Began the first of two tours in Vietnam where he received a commission as a second lieutenant in the U.S. Marine Corps.

1967   Promoted to first lieutenant. He won many medals: the Silver Star, the Bronze Star, two Purple Hearts, the Presidential Regiment Citation, the Navy Commendation Medal, and the Vietnamese Cross of Gallantry.

1968   Returned to Memphis.

1969   Smith took over Arkansas Aviation Sales, Inc. He soon detected a gap in the supply lines of parts and equipment in the growing corporate jet industry. Around the same time, he became frustrated with inept airfreight services. His experiences prompted him to consider the idea of shipping freight on passenger planes, but this idea proved to be impractical for big airlines and he began to think about alternatives.

1970   Smith first became interested in Falcon jets which were fast and small.

1972   Assembled the early staff of Federal Express and started converting Falcons into cargo planes. Due to lack of financial support, he ended up bidding for U.S. Postal Service contracts; by the end of the year, half of the company's $2.8 million income came from handling mail.

1973   Took out loans to finance further expansion and also gained financial backing from two wealthy investors. In January, Smith had 150 employees and an executive office in Memphis, but only nine Falcon jets, all of which were carrying U.S. mail. He needed to free up at least six Falcons to launch Federal Express. After an unsuccessful first run, the second delivery run carried 183 packages.

1974   Business had not taken off yet. One investor pulled out and the company stood on the brink of bankruptcy, even as it continued to expand.

1975   Federal Express finally eked out a $55,000 profit in July and from then on made money.

1976   At this point FedEx employed 1,856 people, flew 37 planes in 82 airports in the United States, and had a payroll of $26.5 million. Net income kept climbing steeply: $3.5 million in 1976, $8.1 million in 1977, $20 million in 1978, and $89 million by 1983. Smith lobbied in Washington for changes in the Federal Aviation Act of 1958 which inhibited cargo carriers from using large aircraft and imposed numerous other restrictions on them.

1977   Changes in the Federal Aviation Act of 1958 allowed cargo carriers to use aircraft of any size and to escape regulatory price control. FedEx promptly bought Boeing 727s and then went public.

1978   Smith played a role in lobbying Congress to lower the capital gains tax, which then saved him millions of dollars.

1980's   FedEx developed regional hubs, altering the concept of the central "hub," which had become inefficient due to the volume of packages. Introduced other innovations including a system for tracking packages.

1990   Won the Department of Commerce's Malcolm Baldrige National Quality Award.

1997   FedEx benefited from growth in their international operations.

FedEx currently is the world's largest express transportation company, with $10 billion revenues in 1996. It employs 127,200 people worldwide and serves approximately 211 countries in 325 airports. Frederick W. Smith remains its chairman, president, and CEO.

SOURCES
1. Wetherbe, James C., *The World On Time: The Management Principles that Made FedEx an Overnight Sensation* (Santa Monica, CA: Knowledge Exchange, 1996).
2. Sigafoos, Robert A., *Absolutely, Positively Overnight: Wall Street's Darling Inside and Up Close* (Memphis, TN: St. Luke's Press, 1983).
3. *FedEx Facts* (http://www.fedex.com/facts).
4. Trimble, Vance, *Overnight Success* (New York: Crown Publishers, Inc., 1993).

Peter Lynch

1944   Born in Boston, Massachusetts.

1955   Started working as a caddy on the golf course for, among others, the president of Fidelity Management & Research. He began to learn about and follow the stock market.

1962   Received his B.A. from Boston College on a golf scholarship. Invested in Flying Tiger stock which surged because of the Vietnam war, giving Lynch enough money to pay his way through graduate school at Wharton.

1963   Fidelity International Fund was started by Ned Johnson, son of Fidelity's founder.

1965   Fidelity International Fund became the Magellan Fund.

1966   Lynch received an M.B.A from Wharton School of Finance at the University of Pennsylvania. He met his future wife, Carolyn, and went to work at Fidelity as a summer intern.

1967   Went into the army for two years.

1969   Returned to Fidelity to work as an analyst covering the textile, metals, chemical, and car industries.

1974   Lynch became Fidelity's director of research.

1976   Fidelity merged the Magellan Fund (which had shriveled from the 1966 holding of $20 million to $6 million) with its $12 million Essex Fund.

1977   Lynch became manager of the Magellan Fund (at the time closed to the public and serving primarily as a repository for investments of Ned Johnson and other

Fidelity executives). Lynch shifted stock selection to his favorite picks, including Congoleum, Transamerica, Union Oil, Aetna Life and Casualty, Hanes, Taco Bell, and Fannie Mae. The total included fewer than 50 stocks.

1977–
1980

Under Lynch's direction, the fund grew in fantastic proportions until the recession of 1980. Between 1978 and 1979, it grew from $26 million to $53 million. It outperformed the Standard & Poor's 500 Index by almost 38% in 1980.

1981

Magellan Fund merged with the smaller Salem Fund and then opened to the public. Investors rushed to pour money into the fund. The fund had passed the $100 million mark in 1980, but the stock market fell apart soon after. Lynch still managed to beat S&P 500 in 1981, but not by nearly as much as in previous years. Lynch divided Magellan's resources among 200 different stocks including supermarkets and fast food chains.

1982

The stock market was not performing well. Lynch invested more and more into Chrysler—up to 5% of Magellan's assets, the maximum percentage allowed. The fund became increasingly popular, reaching $450 million by the end of the year.

1983

Magellan reached $1.6 billion by year end. Its performance ranked first in a five-year reckoning, 200 percentage points above the second-best performer. This success spurred the creation of many different mutual funds by Fidelity.

1987

Magellan had become a $10 billion fund. "Black Monday" did a great deal of damage, but Lynch continued to outperform the market when stocks rebounded.

1989   Published the best-selling book, *One Up On Wall Street: How to Use What You Already Know to Make Money in the Market.*

1990   Lynch retired from Fidelity to spend more time with his family. When he left, Magellan Fund was the largest in the world, with $14 billion in assets.

1992   Lynch agreed to come back to Fidelity, two days a week, to mentor the younger fund managers and become more accessible to the media. His official title was "vice chairman," but he continued to avoid the management aspect of the company.

1993   Published his second highly successful book, *Beating the Street.*

1994   Published his most recent book, *Learn and Earn: A Beginner's Guide to the Basics of Investing and Business.* The book was written by Lynch to educate high school children on the rules of investing.

He currently works for the United Way and the Catholic Charities, raising money for scholarships for inner-city children in Boston and writes frequent articles for *Worth* magazine.

SOURCES
1. Lynch, Peter, *Beating the Street* (New York: Simon & Schuster, 1993).
2. Henriques, Diana B., *Fidelity's World* (New York: Scribner, 1995).

Pleasant Rowland

1962   Graduated from Wells college in upstate New York. Began her career teaching in public and private schools in Massachusetts, Georgia, California, New Jersey (1962–1968). Disappointed with the reading instruction materials available, she created her own.

1968   Landed a job as a television news reporter and anchor at KGO-TV in San Francisco. A story she researched on a new bilingual reading program led her to an educational publisher who was interested in her teaching materials. He offered her a job writing a reading and language arts program for kindergartners.

1971   Pitched her developing program, *Beginning to Read, Write and Listen* to a publisher. It became a best-seller. From 1971 to 1978, Rowland served as vice president of Boston Educational Research Company. She also produced *The Addison-Wesley Reading Program.*

1981   Became publisher of *Children's Magazine Guide*, a library resource that indexes 45 children's magazines. She tripled its circulation and sold it in 1989.

1985   Rowland visited Colonial Williamsburg where she was both impressed by the experience and disenchanted with the quality of educational materials available. She proposed a family guidebook about the Virginia Living History Museum. It was accepted and became highly successful. About the same time, while looking for a gift for a niece, Rowland discovered a gap in the toy market which sparked the idea behind Pleasant Company.

1986   Founded Pleasant Company to market and distribute the American Girls Collection. Geared towards girls ages 7 to 12, the core of original collection consisted primarily of dolls and books distributed through direct mail. Books in The American Girl's Collection bring history alive through the eyes of their 9-year-old heroines who are living in different periods of America's past. The dolls have historically accurate clothing and accessories.

1990   Institute of American Entrepreneurs honored her as one of the nation's twelve outstanding entrepreneurs, from a field of 3000 corporations.

1992   Rowland was appointed to the Board of Directors at the Institute of American Entrepreneurs.

1993   Expanded her brand with *American Girl* magazine which, today, has 670,000 subscribers. *Advertising Age* selected her for its Marketing 100, a list of the "best and brightest" in marketing. Harvard Business School Alumni Club of Wisconsin named her 1993 Business Leader of the Year. *Working Woman* magazine, in cooperation with the National Foundation for Women Business Owners, cited her as one of America's Top 50 Women Business Owners in 1993, 1994, and 1995.

1996   By this time, the company had 600 employees (3000 during Christmas season). It had sold 3 million dolls, 35 million accompanying books, and attracted 675,000 subscribers to *American Girl* magazine.

Rowland has expanded the company to include American Girl of Today Dolls, American Girl Gear, The American Girl's Club, and The American Girl Library. She is a member of the International Women's Forum and the Committee of 200, organizations which honor women of achievement in business.

SOURCES
1. Erickson, Gregory K., *What's Luck Got To Do With It?* (New York: Wiley, 1997).
2. *Background Information: Pleasant T. Rowland Biography* from Pleasant Company Service Department (Middleton, WI: 1997).

Paul Volcker

1927   Born in Cape May, New Jersey. Grew up in Teaneck, New Jersey, where his father was the city manager.

1945   Graduated from Teaneck High School and attended Princeton where he played basketball. He missed the draft because of his height (6'8").

1949   Graduated from Princeton summa cum laude. (Today Volcker is the Frederick H. Schultz Professor of International Economic Policy at Princeton.) That same year he landed a part-time job at the Federal Reserve Board as a research assistant analyzing the supply and demand of money.

1951   Earned an M.A. in political economy and government at Harvard. Worked in Washington as a junior management assistant in the Treasury Department.

1952   Went on to a Rotary scholarship to study at the London School of Economics. Upon his return, he worked with Robert V. Roosa, manager of research for the Federal Reserve Bank of New York. Roosa later became his mentor.

1957   Was convinced by David Rockefeller to become financial economist at Chase Manhattan Bank.

1962   Became director of the Treasury's Office of Financial Analysis at the Treasury Department in Washington.

1963   Kennedy appointed Volcker as an aide to Roosa, who was Undersecretary for Monetary Affairs of the Treasury Department. Volcker helped to avert financial panic when Kennedy was assassinated by closing down the banks and stock exchanges.

1965   Left the Treasury and went to work again for David Rockefeller at Chase as vice president for "forward planning."

1969   Became undersecretary of monetary affairs in the Nixon Treasury.

1971   Was the main architect of Nixon's 1971 plan to eliminate fixed exchange rates for currencies. No longer using gold as a standard, the world monetary system was dismantled and replaced with floating exchange rates. Each of the top ten industrial countries revalued its currency.

1975   Appointed president of the New York Federal Reserve Bank. He also became a member of the policymaking Federal Open Market Committee (FOMC).

1979   Volcker accepted job as Chairman of the Federal Reserve Board under President Jimmy Carter.

1979   Sought to control soaring U.S. inflation. Oil prices had almost doubled in part because the dollar's declining value caused oil companies to jack up prices. People abandoned bonds and bank certificates to invest in gold. Volcker tightened the reins on money flow. He changed Fed policy so that, rather than setting *specific* interest rates, it set up a *range* for interest rates. The Fed kept shifting this range upward as interest rates continued to rise.

1980   Carter's new economic program included a system of credit controls, a policy which Volcker approved while bargaining for budget deficit reduction and which later turned disastrous for the economy. By the end of 1980, inflation was soaring at 12.4% and interest rates neared 20%. The Fed clamped down on interest rates later in the year when the prime interest rate hit 21.5%. Reagan was elected President of the United States.

1981   Inflation fell to 8.9%, but the economy was troubled and slid into the deepest recession since the 1930s. Volcker received pressure to lower interest rates, but did not.

1982   Unemployment climbed to over 10%. By the end of the year, inflation had been curbed to 3.9%, but the deficit worsened.

1983   Volcker was reappointed to a second term. His policies paid off in 1983 and 1984 when the economy started to grow while inflation stayed low.

1985   The dollar had gotten so strong that the trade deficit soared and impeded U.S. growth. Widespread speculation on the dollar occurred, and Volcker sought to restrict the overvalued currency. The dollar sank.

1987   With the dollar continuing to fall, Volcker feared another bout of inflation. He convinced other nations to maintain current exchange levels. He resigned after his second term expired, but the monetary policies and economic strategies he had implemented as Fed Chairman are credited with strengthening the U.S. economy and paving the way for our current economic health. Volcker may best be remembered as the man who "broke the back" of inflation.

1988   Volcker named chairman of the investment banking and advisory firm, James D. Wolfensohn, Inc.

1995   Elevated to CEO of James D. Wolfensohn, Inc.

1966   Named as a director of New York City's Banker's Trust.

Volcker is the head of the international committee charged with recovering from Swiss banks millions of dollars lost by Holocaust victims. He is also a director of Nestle S.A., Prudential

Insurance Company, UAL Corporation, and the American Stock Exchange. He has honorary doctorate degrees from Harvard University, Princeton University, and the London School of Economics.

SOURCES
Neikirk, William R., *Volcker: Portrait of the Money Man* (New York: Congdon & Weed, Inc., 1987).

INDEX